Some Like It Cold

Some Like It Cold

**Surfing the
Malibu of the Midwest**

William Povletich

WISCONSIN HISTORICAL SOCIETY PRESS

Published by the Wisconsin Historical Society Press
Publishers since 1855

The Wisconsin Historical Society helps people connect to the past by collecting, preserving, and sharing stories. Founded in 1846, the Society is one of the nation's finest historical institutions.

wisconsinhistory.org
Order books by phone toll free: (888) 999-1669
Order books online: shop.wisconsinhistory.org
Join the Wisconsin Historical Society: wisconsinhistory.org/membership

Unless otherwise noted, all images are courtesy of Lee and Larry Williams. Images on pages xiv, 60, 118, 176, and 229 are courtesy of Carey "Corky" Henning, and the image on page 222 is courtesy of James Gardner.

Cover photo: The Elbow at Sheboygan, Wisconsin, courtesy of James Gardner

Printed in the United States of America
Cover design and interior typesetting by Biner Design

20 19 18 17 16   1 2 3 4 5

Library of Congress Cataloging-in-Publication Data
Names: Povletich, William, author.
Title: Some like it cold : surfing the Malibu of the Midwest / William Povletich.
Description: Madison, WI : Wisconsin Historical Society Press, 2016.
Identifiers: LCCN 2015040489| ISBN 9780870207464 (paperback) | ISBN 9780870207471 (ebook)
Subjects: LCSH: Williams, Larry (Surfer) | Williams, Lee (Surfer) | Surfers—Wisconsin—Sheboygan—Biography. | Surfing—Michigan, Lake—History. | Sheboygan (Wis.)—Biography. | BISAC: SPORTS & RECREATION / Surfing.
Classification: LCC GV839.65.W47 P68 2016 | DDC 797.3/2092—dc23
LC record available at http://lccn.loc.gov/2015040489

♾ The paper used in this publication meets the minimum requirements of the American National Standard for Information Sciences—Permanence of Paper for Printed Library Materials, ANSI Z39.48–1992.

Contents

Author's Note

It has been said that history is only as accurate as the particular perspective from which it was told. This book comes from the unique perspective of Lee and Larry Williams, who, like great fishermen, understand that any story worth sharing often becomes richer after it has had time to ripen at its own pace and of its own accord from memory.

To summarize, Sheboygan, Wisconsin, is a real place. Lee and Larry Williams are real people. And the events chronicled in this story actually transpired. . . .

But long enough ago that the statute of limitations has since expired.

Prologue

As sunlight cracked the horizon, fog began to lift off the cool water. The village had yet to awaken, but inside the Weather Center Café a few blocks from shore, a lone utility light glowed, indicating the town's first sign of life that day. The uneven light created shadows as the café's owner, Teek Phippen, fumbled in the darkness for his cell phone. The determination of a man in his mid-forties awake at 5:30 in the morning wasn't going to be denied. He soon found his phone under a row of tipped-over paper cups, dialed a number, and waited for the groggy greeting on the other end.

"Waves," Teek whispered into the phone. "Let the rest of the gang know. We've got waves." The phone tree had been activated, and soon Teek would find himself among friends.

Moments later, the snow-covered grass of Deland Park crunched under his feet as he walked from his parked car along Broughton Drive to the shoreline, a mere hundred yards away. He cautiously navigated his way across the ice-covered embankments, further jeopardizing his uncertain balance with a ten-foot longboard under his arm. Standing a solid six feet tall and weighing over two hundred pounds, he conceded that the gusting winds made carrying his longboard feel like "wrestling a giant lizard."

The winds howling at twenty-five miles an hour seemed to freeze what moisture he had in his pores but also generated the waves he hoped to surf, which were crashing violently ashore only a few yards in front of him. Cresting at five feet and then seven, the rolling waves kept growing and multiplying. The water spilling onto the sand resembled the foam of a freshly poured beer. At thirty-four degrees Fahrenheit, the water seemed comfortable compared to the air temperature of two below zero. For Teek and the handful of surfers already surveying the conditions at the water's edge, it was an ideal day to surf.

Riding is best when the weather's the meanest, Teek thought. *And these waves can be just as fierce as anywhere in the world.*

Surfable waves this time of year were rare. The window of opportunity to ride them was even smaller. With a warm front scheduled to arrive later that afternoon, the ideal surfing conditions would soon disappear.

"We ain't getting any younger, boys, and these waves aren't getting any smaller," said Jaime Ziegler, the thirty-something youngster in the group.

Alongside Teek and Jaime stood some of the area's finest surfers, all of whom answered the call to adventure while wriggling into their tight, black wetsuits. Australian Grant Davey, who has often been considered the area's most talented surfer, knew he only had an hour before the responsibilities as the head greenskeeper at the locally owned, world-famous golf course would pull him out of the water. Jim Gardner, adjusting the knit cap on his shaved head, held his camera tightly. He knew the day's conditions would produce some phenomenal photos. Kevin Groh, whose salt-and-pepper sideburns were the only sign he was approaching fifty-something, slipped into his stretched-out, vintage wetsuit, long past its prime. "Comfort over style," he always preached.

Knowing their knees, ankles, and hands would go numb under the fierce conditions in about an hour, the surfers were more determined than ever to race the clock of opportunity. As the last of them tossed their boards into the slush-filled waters, the unofficial patriarchs of the group, Lee and Larry Williams, arrived, pulling their cars alongside the Broughton Drive curb.

Stepping out first was Larry, who looked the part of a lifelong surfer with his Hawaiian print shirt, tiger tattoos wrapped around his arm, and a shark tooth hanging from his neck. A shade under six feet tall, Larry was built like a surfer and remained in good shape though he'd been surfing for more than forty years. As his thinning blond hair whipped into his eyes, he surmised, "It's never a bad day if you're at the beach."

Lee got out of the car and surveyed the scene. He was a good five inches shorter than his brother, and his baggy chocolate brown *Team Blatz* jacket gave little indication he was still hovering around his high school weight of one hundred and fifty pounds. After chugging the last of his beer and adjusting his eyeglasses, Lee slipped the cumbersome wetsuit gloves onto his hands and trudged toward the churning water. He wondered if surfing had been like this in California in the 1940s—not cold, of course, but a pastime embraced by a fairly small group of dedicated folks following their passion.

Within moments, the six grown men in black wetsuits were bobbing on the breaks a quarter-mile from shore, poised to ride the right wave when it presented itself. One by one, they climbed onto their ten-foot boards, balancing themselves by leaning in, arching back and standing tall while the torrential surf propelled them toward shore.

After nearly two hours of ripping up and thrashing through the quagmire of ice-filled Lake Michigan waves, the surfers finally succumbed to the early indications of hypothermia and headed in to shore—their limbs frozen and immobile. Out of the water, they needed to generate heat as quickly as possible, before their core body temperatures dipped below ninety-five degrees. It was November, and the gales had arrived on the Great Lakes with wicked gusts upward of fifty miles an hour. As the sun slid over the horizon, the surfers stabbed their boards into a nearby snowbank, standing them upright and evenly spaced like soldiers at attention. The boards looked like the ones on postcards from a sunny Hawaiian beach, except with snow instead of sand, pine trees instead of palm trees, and a sign that read, "Welcome to Sheboygan, Wisconsin."

While America's Dairyland usually conjures images of cows, cheese, and bratwurst, it is also home to a small but fiercely dedicated surfing culture more than two thousand miles away from the Pacific Ocean. It has become a Mecca to a different breed of surfer—one who prefers the perils of frostbite and icebergs to the unpredictability of shark attacks and turf wars. Thanks to the notoriety generated by the area's elder surfing statesmen, Lee and Larry Williams, the fifty thousand residents of Sheboygan, Wisconsin, have begun to realize surfing on the Great Lakes is feasible and more or less reasonable—especially since their beaches are considered by many to be the number one freshwater surfing destination in the world, affectionately known as the Malibu of the Midwest.

Refusing to succumb to the elements, the surfers huddled around a freshly built bonfire that was already radiating plenty of heat. As the flames' warmth melted away the lake's slush from their wetsuits, they began peeling away the soggy layers and replacing them with dry sweatshirts and jackets. Chattering teeth soon gave way to hearty smiles, especially when Lee reached into a nearby snow bank and said, "What's a bonfire without beer, boys?" Pulling a case of beer from beneath a mound of fresh snow, Lee started tossing cans to his friends, happy to take advantage of Mother Nature's cooler.

Within moments, the group fell into their routine of swapping all-too-familiar surfing stories—tales that, thanks in large part to the beer, had grown into mythic tales of adventure and comedy. Always bringing perspective to the conversations was the group's consummate storyteller, Larry Williams, who couldn't help but express affection for his hometown surfing scene.

"How can you not love surfing here?" he asked the group, somewhat rhetorically. With a dramatic pause, he caressed the tip of his Mako shark tooth necklace. "It definitely wasn't nicknamed The Malibu of the Midwest for its sunshine and bikini babes."

"Who are you kidding?" Lee said. "They're here for the beer." He toasted with his beer can turned upside down, a signal that he needed another. The guys all laughed.

As the sun glistened off the Lake Michigan waters in the bright but still-cold November morning, Jaime, youngest of the Sheboygan surfers, asked, "What exactly inspired you guys to surf the Lakes?"

Lee and Larry smiled at each other. Without missing a beat, Larry said, "Have we got a story for you."

First Wave

Chapter One

Not a day went by during the summer of 1966 when Lee and Larry Williams didn't make the three-block trek from their shared bedroom on Sheboygan's south side to the gravel-covered alleyway between Eighth and Ninth streets along Clara Avenue. Nestled behind a gas station across the street from several corner bars stood a musty, rundown garage. The garage stood among discarded construction materials, rotting yard trimmings, and abandoned vehicle parts. Nobody would've ever guessed it was the center of the Sheboygan surfing universe and home to the Lake Shore Surf Club. But for two thirteen-year-old fraternal twins, the opportunity to stand on the garage's outskirts was worth every minute of their emerging adolescence. The chance to be acknowledged, even just slightly with a glance or a nod, by the local surfers three or four years their senior would justify the endless hours they had spent that summer standing off to the side in silence.

"Go home, you posers," one of the surfers barked from inside the garage. "Don't you have G.I. Joes to bury in the sandbox or something?"

But the insults only strengthened their resolve to become part of the group; any acknowledgment was a sign of progress. Larry whispered to Lee, "Today they call us posers. Tomorrow, we'll be called Lake Shore Surf Club members."

Lee looked away, feeling far less optimistic about their chances.

Only a few weeks earlier, the brothers had been completely ignored during an entire Memorial Day weekend spent standing on the outskirts of the garage. Lee was in it for the opportunity to surf. Larry was in it for the social benefits of hanging out with an older crowd. The Lake Shore Surf Club members were all sun-crazed fools, obsessed with the call of Lake Michigan's surfing wonders. It was a call only a handful of others in Sheboygan answered, including Lee and Larry, since surfing on Lake Michigan was the furthest thing from anybody's mind that summer.

Life in Sheboygan was good then. The streets were clean and crime free. Jobs were plentiful. Families gathered around their RCA television sets to watch *Gomer Pyle* and *Bonanza*. Fathers groomed their modest Midwestern lawns with the latest Bolens Orbit Air power mowers. The General Electric portable dishwasher gave mothers more time to help their children with homework. The nation's unrest generated by the Civil Rights Movement in the South and the escalating Vietnam War seemed

From left to right, Larry Williams, Kevin Groh, Rocky Groh, Lee Williams, and Jeff Schultz in 1968

far away. Sheboygan in the 1960s seemed more like the 1950s—a *Leave it to Beaver* family sitcom.

So it was no surprise that Sheboygan's miniscule surf culture was often misunderstood by adults who thought their teenagers were looking for excuses not to work, much like their counterparts in Malibu, Waikiki, and Tahiti. It had only taken a decade for surfing to capture the imaginations of millions across the country, regardless of how far away they were from the nearest ocean. Kids from inland America read *Gidget,* went to the theaters to keep up with the exploits of Frankie and Annette, and watched the endless array of TV commercials exploiting the romance and adventure of the surfing lifestyle. Names such as Miki "Mickey" Dora, Corky Carroll, Ricky Grigg, and Duke Kahanamoku inspired many of the kids who ran away from home to surf those legendary waves. For Lee and Larry Williams, the mythic exploits of those legendary surfers transported them to the world inside the faded brown garage, outside of which they had already spent the majority of their summer.

Although it was the heart of Sheboygan's surf scene, the garage was nothing special. It was originally a single-story, horse-and-carriage barn with sideways sliding garage doors that allowed the group to fill half of the space with classic Indian, Triumph, and Vincent motorcycles. The other side was stuffed with couches and ratty tapestry rugs. *Surfer Magazine* centerfolds were tacked up across the wall like a patchwork quilt, featuring everything from big monster surfing breaks like the Bonzai pipeline to a serene Makaha sunset. An old record player spun the latest tunes since somebody was always bringing in records that had just arrived via mail order from the coast. Often, the popular songs of the Beach Boys and the Rip Chords were discarded for raw, pseudo-surf music from obscure groups on minor record labels.

When unoccupied, the garage stood silent except for an occasional creaking reminder of its age. As soon as the Lake Shore

Surf Club members arrived, the structure exploded to life like a rambunctious toddler. More often than not, the group arrived with squealing tires and honking horns—a ritual that did little to endear them to the neighbors. The van plastered in surf stickers was hard to ignore when cruising the otherwise quiet avenues of Sheboygan. Bolting through stop signs and crosswalks, they considered pedestrians nothing more than hazards. "If you don't like our driving, stay off the sidewalks," they'd holler.

Never ones to miss the adrenaline rush of near-death, they'd spin their cars into a frantic u-turn just as they were about to miss the turn into the alleyway. Putting themselves on two wheels, exposing the muffler and entire undercarriage with the brakes a-blazing, they would make the vehicle slam down on all four wheels, sliding up to within inches of the rotting wooden garage doors. The smell of smoking brakes served as a pungent reminder of the miraculous stop.

As soon as the car's engine backfired, announcing its temporary resting place, a pack of eighteen-year-old boys pried themselves out of their ride with the grace of cattle caught in an electric fence. Amid the sticky eighty-degree heat, Rocky Groh got out of the car wearing a long-sleeved striped shirt underneath his pea coat, all the while keeping a Camel cigarette balanced on the corner of his mouth and his World War II leather helmet and aviator goggles from obscuring his view.

Next out was Genyk Okolowicz, sporting round John Lennon glasses and a shoulder-length, Jim Morrison haircut that complemented his dark complexion. As the group's resident musician, he was never without his twelve-string acoustic guitar, even when crammed into the backseat of a convertible.

Behind him crawled out Mark Hall in a Hawaiian serape, matching shorts, and tan sandals, implying he had just returned from the islands after blowing "Tiny Bubbles" alongside Don Ho.

With the path cleared between the car's backseat and the garage, Bill Kuitert followed, looking to avoid any obstacle that would risk wrinkling his finely pressed white pants and matching navy-and-white striped sailor shirt. He personified the dysfunction of obsessive-compulsive disorder back when such folks were just considered "neat freaks."

Blessed with all the charisma and panache of an award-winning actor strutting along the red carpet, Tom Ziegler stepped out of the car's passenger side. Adjusting his sunglasses, square-jawed Tom strode into the garage as if avoiding imaginary paparazzi inquiries and photo flashbulbs. Such was the life of Sheboygan's most eligible surfing bachelor.

If the spine-tingling sound of metal-on-metal from the oil-parched driver's side door didn't grab the attention of the two enchanted Williams boys, Randy Grimmer, sporting pork-chop sideburns and a gaucho hat, did. By giving the brothers just the slightest of nods, he sent thrills through their skinny chests. Even if the glance was because he had just caught his car keys in his shirt's breast pocket after tossing them around and over his back or because he still smelled the perfume on his collar from another amazing night with the local supermarket checkout girl, Randy was the boys' newest hero. He might as well have walked around with the letter "S" emblazoned on his chest and a cape billowing in the wind.

When Andy Sommersberger pulled up alongside the convertible in the club's official van—emblazoned on both sides with "Lake Shore Surf Club" hand-painted in bubble letters—it felt like a chunk of the moon fell on top of the brothers. Andy exited the van with the gravitas of a future world leader, completely ignoring Lee and Larry standing in plain view. Instead, he barked into the garage, "Are you butt nuggets going to help me unload the back of this van, or what?"

Andy represented what Sheboygan surfing was all about. He was loud, he was brash, and he was a rebellious leader. With the combination of Hollywood good looks, a well-rounded education, and an ambition that couldn't be quenched, he demanded respect not only from his peers but also from adults, a quality not lost on the group since it was believed he could truly convince a snowman to lie in a tanning bed. Taking guff from nobody, Andy was one of those teenagers who everyone said was "going places," and the Lake Shore Surf Club was his first taste of leadership's intoxicating power.

"If I have to unload these boards by myself, you'll all be riding short boards this afternoon," he said. "The other half of your boards will be floating down the Sheboygan River."

Instantly the six Lake Shore Surf Club members reemerged from inside the garage, two already holding cold cans of Pabst beer. The boys began unloading plywood scraps from the surf van's back doors with military precision, as if they'd performed the maneuver numerous times before.

The lumber was part of a larger course of action that could only be explained as the self-preservation skills of a surfer. Always in need of money, surfers rarely held down jobs since their passion for waves superseded any sort of structured responsibility. So at night, or when the waves were flat, the boys scouted various construction sites around town and when nobody was around, they'd fill the back of their truck with abandoned construction plywood and supplies. When they weren't chasing waves, they spent their free time cutting out skimboards, sanding the edges, and emblazoning them with hand-painted logos and racing stripes. For a whopping twenty-five dollars apiece, they'd sell their boards at nearly a 100 percent profit for beer money.

The Williams brothers watched the plywood scraps getting unloaded as if watching heroes in battle. The fact that the heroes had stolen the wood fueled Lee's and Larry's passion for the

Jack and Mary Williams outside their home in 1976

adventurous lifestyle surfing would bring to their mundane lives growing up between two of Wisconsin's most popular cities— Milwaukee, sixty miles south and Green Bay, sixty miles north.

Located on Sheboygan's south side, the Williams house was modest and cramped compared to those of their friends who grew up north of the Sheboygan River—the unofficial dividing line between the community's haves and have nots. Their father, Jack, was a former Coast Guard submarine rescue diver who had spent the first part of his career in the military welding submerged submarines in the Manitowoc shipyards, outfitted with a big brass bell helmet, canvas suit, and lead boots. He learned his trade operating cranes to unload ships with the Seabees in Guam and the Philippines, and it was there that he also acquired the virtues of discipline and responsibility, qualities he tried to instill in his boys. When he ventured down to the beach with his sons to skip stones or shoot twenty-twos along the abandoned army campgrounds, he always promoted the benefits of living just three blocks west of Lake Michigan.

Lee and Larry's sense of adventure stemmed from their father. In his earlier days, Jack Williams was an aspiring saddle bronc rider with dreams of making it big in the rodeo. When he broke his shoulder only a few days after arriving on the circuit, everyone from the rodeo pooled thirty-five dollars in bus money and told him, "Kid, this isn't for you." With his dreams of being a rodeo star bucked, Jack returned to Sheboygan, where he had been born, to build a new life and family for himself. In recent years Jack had become a first mate on 750-foot ore carriers, delivering coal and ore throughout the Great Lakes. The demanding work schedule kept him traveling for all but a few months a year.

That schedule left the boys to be raised by their mother, Mary. At less than five feet tall and weighing eighty pounds, she was truly a stick of dynamite. She possessed a volatile combination of emotions that were liable to explode if properly ignited. Her lack of size did little to diminish her spirit. After spending an exhausting day dealing with narcissistic doctors and incompetent hospital staff as a nurse's aide, she was never in the mood to tolerate any of her boys' shenanigans. If they looked at her the wrong way or sassed back in the heat of an argument, she stood her ground. The fact Lee and Larry are still alive today is proof that counting to ten in a moment of anger can save lives.

Following one of the more heated arguments between mother and twins, Lee and Larry, freshly graduated from second grade, tried to avenge their punishment by swiping her new pair of shoes. Caught up in anger, they dumped her shoes in the toilet, poured in an entire box of soap powder, and repeatedly flushed until suds and bubbles overflowed into the hallway.

Mary thought she was losing her mind. How could her boys be channeling such evil? Yelling at them to stop only made them laugh louder and flush faster. Instead of intensifying the retaliation, she took a moment and sat down at the dinner table to plot out her next move.

"I'll give you something to laugh about," she shouted to them from across the house. Lee and Larry ignored the threat until she walked down the hallway, grabbed both of them by their arms, and marched them into her bedroom, locking the door behind her. With Mary standing in front of a locked bedroom door, the boys' stopped snickering.

"What's wrong, Mom?" Larry asked in the most innocent of tones.

"I want something to laugh about now, so let's get dressed to go out," she replied.

Mary proceeded to dress her rambunctious boys in outfits of her choosing. Since she was extremely petite, she knew the boys would fit into their new outfits without any problems. Within a few minutes the boys stood aghast, swaddled in dresses, with complementary housecoats and shoes.

"This isn't funny," Larry said.

"Oh, it is for me," she answered. "Now let's go into the kitchen and see what your father thinks of your new outfits."

As the three walked the short distance from the bedroom to the kitchen, the boys' defiance turned to fear as both started to sob. When they were told to sit at the kitchen table for dinner, Jack couldn't guide the soupspoon into his mouth from laughing so hard.

"You two look like a couple of Betty Crockers!" he roared.

For a few moments Lee and Larry continued to bawl, but soon their cries of embarrassment turned into laughter as their father kept cracking jokes at their expense.

"This isn't so bad," Larry snickered. Lee agreed as the two started to play along with Jack's jokes.

Not to be foiled, Mary realized she was losing her grasp of the lesson to be learned and played her next move. "All right, boys. Time to go outside and play!"

Being dressed in women's clothes made that one of the most terrifying statements any mother could make to a couple of young boys. Lee and Larry's laugh party was over. When Mary opened the front door, the laughter and banter of neighborhood children sprinkled into the house. The boys' embarrassment was about to go global. With their luck, a group of their neighborhood friends were playing outside. Any shred of dignity either of the boys possessed was gone. They burst into blubbering sobs, complete with shrieking screams of terror and short, gasping breaths.

"We're sorry, Mom," both blurted repeatedly, as if the more they said it the quicker their actions would be erased off the public record. "We'll never do that again," they were willing to swear under oath. Mary had gotten their attention and more importantly, had reinforced that the house was still a dictatorship under her rule.

Since Lee and Larry's older brothers—John, ten years older, and Tim, seven years older—were already grown and gone, Mary focused on her twins. She made sure the house was always clean, the car always washed, and the grass always cut. Regardless of her work schedule at the hospital, there was never a time three meals weren't waiting for her boys at home. If anyone was late, even by a minute, his meal ticket expired, and he was left to fend for himself.

Being on time was a skill Lee mastered early in life, and he rarely missed a meal. Larry, on the other hand, struggled with an internal clock approximately sixteen minutes behind, a tendency he often blamed on being born second. Thanks to their penchant for sticking together, Larry missed fewer meals than he would have otherwise.

Regardless of Mary's efforts to keep her kids well fed, there were summers when they said they weren't hungry. Little did she or her neighbors realize that the "garden gremlins" plaguing their backyard vegetable plots were actually her sons. After the lights were off in the Williams house and everybody was tucked in bed, Lee and Larry slipped into the warm summer night in search of a midnight snack. Neighbors blamed rabbits, which added to the boys' fun. The fun soon grew into a competition: who could eat the most without getting caught. Even though the neighbors grew suspicious, they couldn't fathom local teenagers doing such a thing. Lee and Larry grew so cocky about not getting caught, they brought their own salt and pepper shakers—stolen from local restaurants, of course. Tomatoes, carrots, green peppers, kohlrabies, and soybeans were fair game when they came into season.

Nobody was a bigger target than Mr. Wakefield, who at eighty-five years old prided himself on being a lifelong gardener and a darn good one at that. His strawberries practically melted in one's mouth. After nearly two months of raiding his gardens, Lee and Larry dug into a feast one night with confidence. While they were passing the salt and pepper shakers and slicing into the ripe berries with their pocket knives, Mr. Wakefield appeared from around the corner of his house wearing nothing but a nightshirt and brandishing a black iron skillet.

"What the hell are you two doing out here?" he raged. "I'm gonna squash you hoodlums like a bug!"

They gawked at him. Stunned into silence. Frozen. But when Mr. Wakefield sprinted toward them, Lee and Larry bolted out of the garden and out of the yard, leaving their salt and pepper shakers behind at the crime scene. Being chased by a cussing old man wielding a frying pan felt surreal to the boys, who ran as fast as they could.

When Lee caught up to Larry at the foot of a chain link fence, he catapulted his brother over to the other side and proceeded to crawl over it with the agility of a spider. Thinking Mr. Wakefield would give up the chase now that they'd cleared the fence, they paused for a second, but the old man's resolve only grew stronger as he tromped closer and closer. When his nightshirt caught on the chain link, he growled at the fence and jerked toward the boys, tearing the fabric in one swift motion. No fence was going to stop him from catching the two raiders who had pillaged his precious fruits and vegetables all summer.

When the brothers sprinted through yet another neighbor's yard, Larry couldn't help but think, "We're athletes. How's he keeping up with us?"

It was clear the old man would not be denied—as the fluttering shreds of white nightshirt hanging on a half-dozen chain link fences made clear. Whenever Lee and Larry jumped a fence, Mr. Wakefield was right behind them.

"He's got to give up eventually," Lee panted.

"He ain't quitting," Larry said. "We've run over four blocks, and I can still hear him cussing."

"Well, maybe it's because you've got tomatoes falling out of your pockets leading him right to us," Lee said. He pointed to the trail of red bulbs fading into the darkness behind them.

After ditching the remaining tomatoes, Lee and Larry ducked into a small, unlocked storage shed just a couple houses from home. After about fifteen minutes of waiting while trying to catch their breath, they opened the door.

"I don't hear him," Larry said.

"He did have on just that night shirt, so chafing may have been an issue," Lee joked.

Once the boys realized the coast was clear, Lee decided they had had enough fun for the night. "We gotta get home," he said. The night sky had begun to lighten, and their dad would be leaving for work any minute. Slinking back into the house, they agreed to find safer forms of entertainment.

They focused on saving enough of their allowances to buy a pair of matching skimboards from the Lake Shore Surf Club, and they began dividing their summer days between the beach and the garage. They spent their mornings darting across the foamy edges of Lake Michigan's breaking waves on bullet-shaped plywood. Skimboards were a lot less stable and maneuverable than surfboards because they were smaller and lacked skegs—fins on the bottom used for controlling direction.

Like many surfers before and after them, Lee and Larry used skimboarding to learn the basics of riding waves. It provided an inexpensive way to grab an adrenaline rush that, although a bit shorter, was almost as intense as the one surfers thrived on. Standing approximately twenty feet from the water, they would wait for their waves. When one ominously surged above the horizon, they'd race toward the water's edge with boards in hand, as if to joust the oncoming wave. Upon reaching the wet sand, they'd drop their boards while jumping onto them as quickly as possible in mid-stride. If they managed to get the board under their feet without wiping out, they'd skim across the thin layer of moisture above the water-soaked sand. Literally slipping across the slick film of water, they tried to keep their balance while transitioning onto the oncoming wave. Combining a series of tricks on the wave, from skimming over, banking off, and riding it back into shore, Lee and Larry had tasted the potentially addictive endorphins ignited by gliding across a mountain of water.

By the Fourth of July, the brothers were often joined outside the Lake Shore Surf Club's garage by a group of friends from their junior high school, including Rocky Groh's younger brother, Kevin. Kevin had been a friend of the Williams brothers since kindergarten and was often referred to as the third twin by their parents. The previous summer, the three of them had become tired of older kids constantly kicking over their sand castles and beach forts. Kevin decided to exact revenge by burying concrete bricks underneath and walk away. When one of the older guys would walk by to kick over their creation, he got quite a surprise. Often a yelp of pain was followed by a circus of cuss words while he limped away, no longer looking cool as he tried to catch up with his friends.

Kevin also provided the litmus test for gauging the danger level of a stunt. If he managed to injure himself, but not die, it was worth trying. One summer when Kevin, Lee, and Larry were in elementary school, they ventured over to Motorville, a shop that specialized in selling motorboats and Volkswagen cars. In back by the dumpsters they found abandoned boxes from recently sold outboard motors. Never one to miss an opportunity, the boys dragged the orphaned boxes to the nearby sledding hill that ascended at a steep angle from the foot of the beach. However, in July there was no snow, only dry and prickly grass. Lee and Larry coaxed Kevin to take the first ride down the hill on one of the cardboard boxes. Peering down the steep hill, Kevin was unsure but eventually agreed. He took a running start with his box and slid down the hill, going so fast it seemed his makeshift sled would burst into flames. When he made it to the bottom of the hill without combusting or breaking his neck, Lee and Larry raced each other down on their cardboard toboggans to meet him, knowing they had nothing to fear. Daredevil Kevin had proven his mettle many times and when the boys began their skimboard phase, Kevin was right there with them. They would duel each other, performing outlandish tricks to see who could slide along the shore doing the most eclectic combination of 360s, ollies, fire hydrants, flyaways, coffins, bomb drops, and headstands. When the waves were too big and choppy to skim, they'd use their boards as bodyboards for surfing into the shore break.

They spent most mornings trying out their stunts. In those days before waterproof watches, it was a miracle Lee and Larry didn't miss more lunches that summer. Following their daily pilgrimage home for lunch, the brothers often spent their after-noons hanging out in the dusty alleyway next to the Lake Shore Surf Club's garage. But instead of standing alone, they were often joined by Kevin, who didn't help draw interest from the older guys despite his brother being one of them. Nor did their newly earned status as accomplished skimboarders.

While the rest of Wisconsin's teenage boys seemed to be caught up in Vince Lombardi's Green Bay Packers, souped-up sports cars, and big-game hunting, Kevin and the Williams broth-ers were mesmerized by the Lake Shore Surf Clubbers and what the group represented—a lifestyle born in far-away places like Oahu, Bora Bora, and New Guinea.

Together, they patiently hung around outside the club's ga-rage, killing time while hoping to get invited inside for the chance to help sand skimboards, jam to Jan and Dean on the radio, or swap Lake Shore Surf Club jacket patches—the group's ultimate symbol of acceptance. Maybe if they were in the right spot at the right time, Genyk Okolowicz would ask them to carry his

The coveted Lake Shore Surf Club patch

acoustic guitar into the garage after he wowed a group of teenage girls with his poetry and guitar riffs. Andy might need them to carry in pieces of stolen plywood, or Tom could be a hand short with the Friday night keg.

But such opportunities for servitude never arose, and the boys would eventually leave to focus on how to acquire an actual longboard, which would increase their status within the surfing circle. But between them, they were flat broke and a decent, new surfboard would cost well over one hundred and fifty dollars.

Although emulating the club members in any way possible—from their clothes, their slang, and their music to their style of pushing the limits on the beach—Lee, Larry, and Kevin knew they couldn't consider themselves surfers until somebody else referred to them that way. So like most budding surfers, they would have to abide by the maverick laws that governed the Lake Shore Surf Club.

Sheboygan's surfing community—like so many around the world—made its own rules and hierarchy in which the better surfers enjoyed the greater fruits of the lifestyle. Andy Sommersberger was king of the Lake Shore Surf Club pyramid of power. Everyone else ranked below him. If word came down from Andy on any issue, it was recognized as law. His strictest rule was never to disrespect anyone who ranked higher in the hierarchy. If someone didn't figure out that simple fact fast enough, he suffered some public embarrassment. The first offense often earned a slap behind the ear and a warning to straighten up. A second offense warranted getting stuffed into a garbage can or dropped off in some field in the middle of nowhere, wearing only his skivvies, with no way to get home. That was the law on the beach and nobody questioned it.

Accepting the rules and the hierarchy was part of being a member of the club—as was receiving a nickname. Anyone who surfed long enough or was crazy enough within the Lake Shore

Surf Club circles was given one. Nicknames were earned and couldn't be self-applied. Andy was called "Garbage" for being such a trash talker and for being able to eat anything, especially on a dare. There was also Tom "Tommy Z" Ziegler, a simple nickname that was intoxicating to the ladies. Bill Kuitert was called "Wipeout Willie," more for the alliteration than his surfing style. Riding the hottest noserider model at the time, Randy "Weber" Grimmer was nicknamed after the famous surfboard's designer, Dewey Weber. Until Andy recognized them as surfers or they got nicknames, Larry, Lee, and Kevin would be nothing but annoying gremmies—surfer slang for an inexperienced wannabe.

Whenever they saw Andy Sommersberger bolting around town in his old red Dodge van with big white Lake Shore Surf Club letters painted on the sides, tires jacked up in the back and decked out surfboards tied on top, the Williams boys recognized how he epitomized what California surfing was all about. If they felt for a moment that they, too, were part of that culture, Andy put them in their place by not offering so much as a casual wave or even a glance, leaving them behind in a cloud of green exhaust.

Lee, Larry, and Kevin felt they were surfers on the inside, but they wanted to know what it took to be accepted as a surfer on the outside. Andy, Tom, Randy, and the rest of the club often tried to draw attention to their outlaw status by wearing something outrageous—German World War II helmets, floppy sombreros, or straw hats—and the younger boys did the same. But no matter what kooky ensemble Kevin, Lee, or Larry pulled from their closets, they were never noticed standing outside the garage. And then, just when they were ready to give up hope of recognition, they caught a break.

Kevin's older brother, Rocky, covertly invited them to their first Lake Shore Surf Club party. "Just know your role and don't screw it up for all of us," Rocky warned Kevin. The three were invited to hang out, but only to speak when spoken to and only to enter the water when the older members were too distracted with their beer and their girlfriends to notice.

That night, the excited trio traipsed to Optenburg's Iron Works Beach and were awed by the scene. Hypnotized by it. Bonfires blazed in three separate fire pits, forming an inner circle of mayhem. The sounds of the party—girls shrieking, guys roaring, tires squealing, and electric guitars blaring out of car stereos—would've prompted neighbors to call the police, except that this uninhabited corner of Sheboygan was well out of sight from passing traffic and inquisitive cops.

Engines revved, tires screeched, and headlights appeared out of the darkness. A parade of '57 Chevy Bel-Airs, Nomads, paneled '56 Ford station wagons, and '50 Oldsmobiles with surfboards hanging out of the trunk skidded into curbside parking spots, quickly filling both sides of the street. The ominous shadow of a rusty Dodge van hissed down the street, knocking over two municipal trash cans as it came to a smoldering halt against the curb. Andy Sommersberger jumped out, orphaning the surfboard in the passenger seat. From the back seat, Tom Ziegler appeared, followed by a six-pack of giggling girls. As Andy and Tom followed the girls toward the party, Lee, Larry and Kevin watched from atop a nearby sand dune, silently taking in the entire scene.

"Are those guys boss or what?" Larry asked.

"They sure know how to host a hooter," Lee answered, trying to sound as cool as the older guys.

Tanned honeys and drunken surfers writhed the Watusi to the sounds of Chuck Berry, Little Richard, Fats Domino, the Shirelles, the Four Seasons, the Coasters, Bo Diddley, and Elvis. When the tunes slowed to make-out music—Johnny Mathis, the Platters, and Andy Williams—they clung to each other like magnets.

Even though the party had been raging since dusk, no fights broke out, only the occasional drunken debate over who won the last chugalug contest. The more drunk the partiers got, the more they flopped onto the shabby couches dragged onto the sand, making out and grabbing and groping in ways that Frankie and Annette never did in movies like *Beach Blanket Bingo*.

Even when Randy Grimmer, crooked German helmet and all, fiendishly grabbed hold of the keg spigot and rained beer down on the hordes of people in front of him, nobody even flinched as their sweaty bodies continued to move, groove, and grind to the music.

Lee, Larry, and Kevin had been perched on the dune for almost three hours. For Lee, the excitement of being invited to watch the party from afar began to wear off, and he finally said, "I'm heading home."

"But this is the party of the year," Larry said. "Who knows when we'll be invited back?"

"You call this being invited?" Lee shot back. "Maybe if we're really lucky they'll ask us to clean up after them."

"But this is the surfing lifestyle."

"Then where's the surfing? All I see is us sitting on a pile of sand like seagulls waiting to get fed. Surfing is about getting on a board. You can have the lifestyle." Lee sauntered away, heading off toward home in the warm summer air.

Larry watched him go before calling out, "I'm here whenever they invite me. This is the place to be, man."

On the sand, the flowing beer and rocking music kept everyone in a frothy, romantic mood. Andy Sommersberger, Mark Hall, and Bill Kuitert were ankle deep in sand, dancing slowly, pressed against their dates. Tom Ziegler was making out with a local Betty on the sand-covered couch. Randy had finally crashed out, peacefully snoozing alongside that same sand-covered couch. While Genyk let the Platters' ballad play, he quietly strummed along with his acoustic guitar for a small audience of love-struck girls.

When the party quietly slipped from the beach into the catacombs of the Sheboygan neighborhoods around midnight,

Kevin and Larry kept quietly perched, hoping to get invited to one of the after-parties. The closest they got was when a few slumping and stumbling members gave them drunken shout-outs of "Hey man," or "Dude, what a helluva party."

When Tommy Ziegler, who looked like the twin brother of international surfing sensation Miki Dora, strode by with an armful of ladies, Larry and Kevin perked up, but were once again completely ignored as the posse ventured a few blocks south into a local bar. For Tommy, the party was just getting started as he proceeded to jump on stage with the band to sing along on a few songs. When he wasn't riffing on stage, he was tearing up the dance floor, wooing women with his smooth moves. By the end of the night, he'd have two older women hanging off his arms. But no matter how late he was out partying, Tom was sure to be in the water surfing the next morning. Kevin, Lee, and Larry would be there too.

The trio sat atop the sand dune with a clear view of the Lake Michigan shore. The entire Lake Shore Surf Club was in the water, seemingly recovered from the previous night's hedonism. Tom was as graceful riding a wave that morning as he had been on the dance floor a few hours earlier. He was cross-stepping and nose riding while tearing up the waves with a laid back style nobody could touch. Never raising his hands above his waist or placing his feet farther apart than his shoulders, Tom was flawless on the board, no matter the size or chop of the wave. Among the Sheboygan surfers, he was considered the best longboarder on the local surf circuit.

After an hour of taking in the scene, Lee, Larry, and Kevin saw Rocky heading down to catch his first waves of the morning. Under his arm was a new Con Ugly Noserider Surfboard that he had bought recently for an astronomical two hundred and thirty-eight dollars. At the time, that was a lot of money. You could buy a real good junker of a car for only five hundred bucks. But none of his friends thought Rocky was crazy after capturing their first wave on the new board. America agreed. That two-foot-wide board with a flexible nose quickly became the number one nose-riding board in the country.

And it was about to send three boys on the ride of their lives. Noticing them sitting patiently, Rocky trotted over to them. "You want to take it out?" he asked.

"Us?" Larry replied. He was stunned.

"What's the catch?" Lee asked.

Rocky shrugged. "Just trying to be nice to my brother and his friends. You've been hanging around us long enough to deserve a chance to prove yourselves."

The boys all looked at each other, still unsure whether Rocky was playing a joke.

Rocky said, "Hey, I can't surf today anyway." Earlier in the week, when there wasn't any surf, Andy Sommersberger and the boys had taken their motorboat onto the water to tow the surfboards—sort of a makeshift water-skiing/surfing excursion. Rocky's wetsuit had been in the bottom of the boat soaking in a puddle of gasoline. When Rocky put the wetsuit on the next morning, he quickly got a full-body, bright-red rash. The pain was excruciating. It was a small price to pay for a bunch of adrenaline junkies looking to push the envelope whenever possible.

By the time Kevin, Larry, and Lee decided to accept the invitation, Rocky's board sat perched in the sand, on the outskirts of the Lake Shore Surf Club's temporary beach camp of towels and coolers. Kevin approached the board like a first-time cat burglar, knowing he could be scolded at any moment for even entertaining the thought of surfing alongside Andy, Tommy, and the rest. Hoping not to be noticed, Lee and Larry stepped off the sand dune, following about fifty yards behind Kevin, who nervously lugged the board toward the shoreline. None of the guys in the water noticed him, focused instead on keeping their balance in the thrashing waves.

Kevin hit the water with Lee and Larry right behind him, all of them waiting for their fantasy to end with a harsh comment from the older guys. Instead, they found the Lake Shore surfers going about their business, completely uninterested in the boys down shore.

The trio spent the rest of the morning teaching themselves the nuances of balancing atop the longboard while navigating some pretty intimidating waves. Although they never lasted more than a handful of seconds atop the board, it was enough to experience the adrenaline rush that only surfing can evoke in a man's soul.

As Lee, Larry, and Kevin paddled out into the Lake Michigan surf, they were about to realize the importance of respect—in this case, respect for the wave—by being taught their first of many life lessons through surfing. Each of them ignored their fear of the unknown as they came closer to the waves' intoxicating impact zone. They discarded their goal of catching a manageable wave to surf, exchanging that goal for the glory they could achieve by surfing the largest of arcing barrels, despite their inexperience. After being thrashed around by several waves, where nature's law of survival of the fittest plays no favorites, they took a more rational approach when the next set of white-tipped waves approached. When the initial endorphin rush gave way to other sensations, their fears subsided, allowing them to communicate with the swells, sensing the rhythm and natural language of the waves. That morning, the three boys were introduced to the deeper meaning of what it meant to be on a lifelong quest for the perfect wave, as only a surfer atop a wave on a surfboard can truly experience.

The following week, Kevin, Lee, and Larry continued to hang around the Lake Shore Surf Club, thinking they had, at last, earned attention as legitimate surfers. No dice. They were as invisible as they'd been before.

Lee had suffered long enough. "I'm out," he told Larry and Kevin. "You can spend the rest of your summer standing outside this garage or chasing these guys around, but I've got better stuff to do with my time."

"But we're so close to being accepted," Larry said. "And we never would've got to ride Rocky's board if we hadn't put our time in."

"Rocky would never admit it," Kevin said, "but these guys like having us around. Their girlfriends dig how they let us be their charity cases."

"Let's go ahead and ask them to let us be members," Larry said.

Lee shook his head. He didn't want to be there to watch them wipe the floor with his eager brother. He wanted to be acknowledged as a surfer but he had his pride, too.

Following an awkward silence, the boys decided to go home for the day. They walked back without saying a word, each of them thinking about how to resolve the situation. School would start again in a few weeks, and they'd spent the entire summer trying to be surfers.

The next morning, Larry awoke with the roosters as the sun peeked over the glassy waters of Lake Michigan. He jumped out of bed and ventured down to the garage alone. As a man on a mission, he dismissed Lee's theory of never being accepted into the group as nothing more than a lack of effort. The only reason they weren't members yet was because they hadn't outright asked. Shyness was for wimps.

Marching down the alleyway, Larry kept talking through the script, determining everyone's responses. He had imagined the conversation with Andy, Tom, and Randy all night, a process that kept him awake into the wee hours of the morning. By the time he walked into the garage, his membership request had been universally accepted in his own mind with a hearty "Welcome to the club, Larry, and here's your honorary patch."

Instead, Andy Sommersberger, who had been crashed out on the couch until awakened by the creaking door, peeked with one eye open and growled, "Who let you in here, gremmie?"

Still confident but caught slightly off guard by Andy's aggression, Larry stuck to his script. "We want to become members of the Lake Shore Surf Club."

Without pause, Andy fired back, "Get out, you snot-nosed punk. Who do you think you are asking to be a member of our club?"

"We've spent the entire summer hanging out, just waiting to become part of the Sheboygan surfing scene," Larry said, his voice cracking just slightly. "We've earned the chance."

"The club is no place for a bunch of bare-chested kids. There's too much drinking and womanizing going on. You don't even have your driver's licenses yet."

The last snipe silenced Larry, who lowered his head and moped out of the garage. It was clear, even to the ever-hopeful Larry, that the club would never acknowledge them as surfers or let them join. He slowly shuffled his way back home, feeling that everything he'd done all summer was, as Lee said, a complete waste of time.

When he got home he told Lee about the conversation, including the qualifier about obtaining driver's licenses, which was still two long years away. Larry admitted Lee had been right all along and prepared himself for an I-told-you-so.

Instead, Lee said, "Why can't we form our own surf club? Who says they own the exclusive rights to surfing in Sheboygan?"

Larry perked right up. Of course. If they couldn't join the cool club they'd start a new one. And by the end of the conversation, the Great Lakes Surf Club was born.

Chapter Two

Modeling their creation after the Lake Shore Surf Club, Lee and Larry began recruiting a handful of friends. Some had aspirations, like Lee and Larry, of one day being accepted by the Lake Shore Surf Club. Others were just looking for something exciting to do during the remaining dog days of August before school started.

The group's first official member was Kevin Groh, and they quickly grew to about two-dozen strong. Unlike the Lake Shore gang, the Great Lakes Surf Club not only accepted, but actually encouraged girls to join. The boys figured the club needed the extra revenue from memberships, and the offer was also a great excuse to spark up a conversation with a cutie. Much to their surprise, the local girls thought it was cool to be part of a surf club. Within a week of hatching their idea, the Great Lakes Surf Club was hosting its own nightly bonfires at the beach. By partying around the same fire pit, near the same sand dune every night, kids in search of their friends knew where the action would be.

The excitement Lee and Larry cultivated for the Great Lakes Surf Club spilled into the start of the school year. During lunch, while most of their classmates hung out on the playground, shot hoops, or played kickball, Lee, Larry, and a handful of friends took advantage of the open-campus policy by sprinting the two blocks from Farnsworth Junior High School to the beach. Picking up their skimboards along the way, they'd spend the entire lunch hour riding waves. Because the dress code prohibited them from wearing shorts to school, they'd board with their jeans on rather than waste time changing clothes. Often they returned to school right before the final bell and sat at their desks dripping water and sand on the floor below them. Although frustrated beyond words, the teachers could only grit their teeth in silence since no dress code rules were technically broken.

And while Lee and Larry never viewed themselves as any more eccentric than most teenagers, they did manage to draw the wrath of teachers about actual dress code violations. Walking the halls wearing Chuck Taylor high-tops without socks, a Tiki necklace, and a surf t-shirt underneath a tattered army jacket, they were easy targets. But as the rebels they tried to be, as soon as they got out of view they were strutting and untucking.

One wardrobe item that got Larry hauled to the principal's office was the surfer's cross around his neck. Worn as a talisman to bring good waves to surfers, the cross was also an anti-establishment symbol that distinguished them from the rest of society. Based on the German Iron Cross, it featured a surfer riding a board in the middle of the cross's front side. After being yanked out of class and accused of being a Nazi sympathizer, Larry was left to explain himself or receive a punishment. Pulling out the most recent issue of *Surfer Magazine* from his back pocket, he opened to an advertisement. "Ya see? Right there. That's a surfer's cross. What I'm wearing is a surfer's cross. I'm a surfer, not a kraut-sucking Nazi."

Academics quickly became secondary to the boys as the Great Lakes Surf Club's first official order of business was to raise money to buy some jackets, patches, and surfboards—all items needed to legitimize their organization in the eyes of others. Despite not having their driver's licenses yet, they were able to organize a car wash in a local grocery store parking lot. While a lot of the cars didn't quite get the thorough washings as advertised, they certainly did get a lot of driving miles on them. The kids eagerly hopped into people's cars and drove around the parking lot a few extra times before getting in line for the washing. The fundraiser was a big success, and by the end of the day, the Great Lakes Surf Club had accumulated over one hundred and fifty dollars in seed money.

With the funds in hand, the boys didn't have to look far for inspiration on the design for their orange Great Lakes Surf Club jackets. The local car club in town, the Sandmen, sported Nehru jackets with a palm tree and sunset embroidered on the back. Since they were driving some of the sweetest hot rods around and all dated good-looking women, the Sandmen were the perfect model. So for a handful of teenage boys, the choice was obvious—Nehru jackets with the simple letters GLSC on the back and a Great Lakes Surf Club patch sewn on the left breast. Now the group was not only an excuse to hang out together and party, but also an excuse to wear a really cool club jacket around town.

With their remaining car wash funds, the Great Lakes Surf Club decided to rent their own garage. Thanks to a friend of the family, Lee and Larry found a place where the group could hang out and house their growing collection of skimboards. For five bucks a month they enjoyed the perfect place for a bunch of teenagers on the verge of high school to experience the joys and sorrows of adolescence in Sheboygan. Many nights found a dozen guys on the garage floor covered in sleeping bags, planning to get a jump on the morning surf. Each boy would tell his parents he was sleeping at somebody else's house, and then they'd secretly gather in the garage. The boys' late night conversations often focused on how they could get longboards, the novelty of skimboarding having faded.

Lee and Larry decided it was time to take part-time jobs. Although Lee, as the fiscally responsible brother, had built up quite a war chest from months of saving his dollar-a-week allowance,

Larry chewed through cash as if it were coated in bubble gum. With disposable income scarce around the Williams house, only the anticipation of owning their own surfboards kept the boys focused on their new jobs—Lee delivering afternoon newspapers and Larry raking leaves in the autumn before clearing away neighborhood sidewalks with a snow shovel in the winter for a buck per house.

After several blizzards, numerous days of sub-zero wind chills, and endless cloudy skies, the Williamses were stoked when Sheboygan's surf season kicked into full gear around the year-end holidays.

One afternoon on his daily paper route, Lee saw a surfboard parked against a garage—a California-style board wedged into a Sheboygan snow bank was a bizarre sight, and he needed to check it out. He approached the front door with a gleam in his eye. A young, fit, and tanned surfer answered the door wearing floral-patterned board-shorts and a University of Southern California sweatshirt. Looking for an icebreaker, Lee said he had knocked in order to thank the household for being such loyal customers of the *Sheboygan Press* newspaper, but he soon led the conversation into surfing, especially the differences between Santa Monica and Sheboygan wave riding. Lee quickly gained the college student's trust by showing his knowledge of the sport went well beyond casual. Once he felt comfortable, Lee asked the guy, who was home for the holidays, "In the spirit of the season, can I rent your surfboard?"

"Sure," the student said. "And in the spirit of the season, it'll only cost you twenty-five cents an hour." A square deal if Lee had ever heard one. "When you're done," the student added, "put it back in the garage and leave the money by the board."

Every day for the next two weeks, Lee made that house the last stop on his route, picking up the board and heading for the beach with his brother. For a kid making fourteen dollars a week on his route, dropping two bits an hour to rent a board was the best deal in town.

Although Lee and Larry had surfed on a few longboards before, this one was different. Maybe it was because they didn't have to immediately hand it off to someone else after each run. Maybe it was because they were renting it, as opposed to borrowing. Or since they had all day to surf without worrying about only having one chance to get in a good run, they enjoyed a sense of ownership. The slush-topped Lake Michigan waves did little to keep them from improving their surfing skills.

Dressed in blue jeans, sweatshirts, and cotton gloves, they took a couple of practice runs on the sand before paddling out a quarter-mile to the first favorable break, where they took turns riding the board on their knees back to shore. When they tried to stand up, the first wave's momentum sucked the board toward shore, leaving them to practice their retrieval skills since the board was without a leash.

Knowing their task would've been easier if the board had been resting on a solid surface, they kept trying to make their leap from a prone position in the water coincide with the board as it constantly shifted above the lurching surge of swirling water. When they actually got their feet planted on the board firmly enough to stand, they then battled gravity's unforgiving forces while weighting and unweighting left, right, front, and back—whatever it took to keep from plunging into the watery abyss below. All too often it resulted in a losing combination.

It has been said that learning how to surf is like learning to ride a bicycle. Fighting the urge to walk away after several face-plant dismounts, one must try again and again while listening to no end of advice from people who have done it. And then, just when failure has almost convinced ambition that there is no way someone can stand upright on a surfboard for more than a few seconds, "it" clicks.

And that's how it was for Lee and Larry. The trick of landing the board suddenly came together, and soon they were standing atop two-foot waves, gracefully gliding toward the Sheboygan shoreline. Although they had spent endless hours swimming, bodysurfing, and skimboarding Lake Michigan's waves, the euphoria of "Oh my God, I can do this" shone in their faces from atop their first wave. It was a threshold they'd crossed, knowing what was once an adolescent curiosity had turned into a life's passion.

For the rest of their holiday break, Lee and Larry spent every spare minute at the beach on their rented surfboard, mostly by themselves, though sometimes Kevin Groh and other hearty Great Lakes Surf Club members tried to get in a couple of rides with Sheboygan's newest surfing sensations. By the end of the two-week vacation, Lee and Larry had racked up nearly ten dollars in rental fees at a quarter an hour.

For a couple months after the owner of the surfboard returned to USC, Lee and Larry suffered from the shakes like a couple of dried-out alcoholics. They needed to buy a board of their own. And so they searched the local classified ads for a used surfboard with no success until one glorious day when they read, "Ten foot wooden hollow surfboard, spar varnished with marine shellac—$25."

The tiny ad in the Sunday classifieds seemed to melt the snow piled on the kitchen windowsills and make the sun shine brighter through the frost-covered windows. Before Larry had even finished reading the ad, Lee had begun dialing the phone number to arrange a time to pick up the board. The next twenty-four hours were some of the most anxiety-filled moments of their lives. They would soon be owners of their very own longboard.

The next day, Lee completed his paper route in record time. He had gotten a head start after meeting the *Sheboygan Press* delivery truck outside his house, dropping the stack of newspapers directly into his bicycle basket, and not once letting up on his pedaling. When he tossed his last paper onto the neighbor's lawn he raced back to the house to pick up Larry. It was time to meet their new board.

They pedaled their bikes as quickly as possible through the labyrinth of Sheboygan sidewalks and alleyways inland to the address listed in the classified ad. Escorted into the garage by the board's owner, they couldn't see a thing until the guy turned on an overhead utility light that shone upon a cluttered maze of boxes, worn-out lawn equipment, and broken bicycles. Tucked away in the garage's dusty shadows, behind a rusted pickup truck on sawbucks, stood the shellacked piece of marine plywood. It resembled an ancient Hawaiian board the boys had read about but never actually seen in person. As advertised, the ten-foot-long wooden hollow surfboard was varnished with industrial shellac, was five inches thick, and had a rubber plug in the nose with a big wooden rudder on the bottom. It wasn't one of those sleek, airplane-winged boards, but rather what Hawaiian surf historians often called a cigar box or kook box. It was similar to the boards the biggest names in the history of surfing started out with—big old wooden planks that needed two or three neighborhood kids to carry to the beach.

Forking over the money, Lee and Larry were head-over-heels in love, though they had no idea how they would get it home on their bikes. They headed directly to the beach, holding their new purchase as they pedaled their bikes in tandem without losing their balance or dropping the board onto the pavement.

It wasn't until they placed the board into the water that they discovered why it was so reasonably priced. As soon as the first wave washed over the board, it began taking on water like a sieve and proceeded to sink. Full of water, it easily weighed more than one hundred pounds. Only pride in their new purchase kept them from abandoning their sinking log on the spot.

Dressed in denim jeans and sweatshirts, they endured the twenty-degree air temperatures while wading in forty-degree waters, ignoring the early signs of hypothermia setting in as their lips turned purple and extremities began to swell. After a couple of hours of trying to stand on the board, the two realized their clothes did nothing but exacerbate the numbing cold and prevent them from balancing themselves.

Upon returning home and thawing out in front of the fireplace, Lee and Larry decided to make an even stronger commitment toward their love of surfing. For twenty-five dollars apiece, they purchased wetsuits. The modified SCUBA suits were bulky, awkward, and nearly three-quarters of an inch thick with the interior velour liner. Manufactured for warm weather excursions in places like the Caribbean, the suits had short sleeves and short pants, leaving arms and legs exposed to Lake Michigan's unforgiving elements. That posed a serious problem for Lee and Larry since they found it nearly impossible to stay balanced on a surfboard, especially without the ability to feel their knees and ankles.

When the wetsuits arrived, everything seemed to leak. Since the pants came up to their chests and the jacket came down almost past their hips, they taped the seams of their gloves and boots in hopes of making a seal. To combat the accumulating water around their feet, they wore socks, which only weighed them down like cement blocks tied to their ankles. Even when they thought they had created a perfect seal, the suit's big beavertail—basically a crotch flap with turnbuckles—would always fail during a big wipeout. If a wave jettisoned them at the right angle, the wetsuit would unhinge, roll up to their chest, and practically straightjacket them. It was quite the visual metaphor for the

Larry stays ahead of the breaking surf in 1970, despite the dragging beaver-tail on his wetsuit.

brothers' efforts since they were crazy enough to even consider surfing in Lake Michigan's frigid winter waters in the first place.

They'd wear hoods to cover their shoulders and necks, with a small hole from the top of the eyebrows down to the bottom of their lips to minimize exposure, but this presented another problem. They needed to be able to turn their heads to cut and swing around the faces of waves.

Riding the waves with their own board became almost as frustrating as it was fun.

Lee and Larry took out their frustrations on their board by abandoning it on the beach each night when they were finished surfing. Why go through the trouble of lugging it back and forth from home? Who would try to take it? The board was too heavy to steal and a lot of people didn't even know exactly what it was. Those who did know weren't stupid enough to try riding it because any sane person knew the water was too damn cold.

As proof that their obsession with the beach had become a year-round affair, Lee and Larry transitioned from sporting summer sunburns to wicked winter windburns. Often, it seemed as if they were making up for lost time; it had only been four years since they were allowed to visit the water unsupervised for the first time.

Though the Williams family lived only three blocks from the water on Ninth Street, their parents forbade them from crossing Eighth Street. One of the busiest and most treacherous streets to cross in Sheboygan, especially for an unsupervised child, Eighth Street presented an imposing obstacle and made visiting the beach on their own as unlikely as a trip to the moon. But after years of persistent nagging, they wore down their parents.

"When you turn ten, you'll be old enough and responsible enough to cross the street on your own," their mom had said.

When dawn broke on November 5, 1963, Larry leaped out of bed before the first ray of sunshine hit his pillow. With an extra jump in his step, he put a leash on the family's little Pomeranian dog and was out the door within five minutes. The two strutted along the sidewalk, heading straight down Georgia Avenue toward the beach. Nothing would keep him from crossing Eighth Street that morning because he had just turned ten. As if destiny were playing in his favor, Larry walked up to the crosswalk right as the light turned green, not even having to break stride to venture across Eighth Street for the first time all on his own.

He spent the entire morning wandering the Lake Michigan shoreline with a new sense of empowerment and discovery. From countless hours of reading surf magazines, he realized for the first time that Sheboygan was in the best location for surfing anywhere on the Great Lakes. Understanding that surfers are only restricted by geographical necessity (a coastline that generates sizeable waves), he no longer saw a series of river mouths, rocky outcroppings, piers, jetties, sandbars, and a reef one mile offshore, but rather twenty-two different breaks over a five-mile stretch that with a surfboard could be conquered like never before.

Lake Michigan waves don't have thousands of miles to build up like ocean waves do, and so wind speed and fetch—the area of surface where the wind generates the waves' swell—are two key elements that contribute to surfable waves. Because Sheboygan County juts out five miles into Lake Michigan, winds from most directions cause water to swell. The third factor concerns where the wave meets the shore in a fated climax known as a break. Between Sheboygan's mile-long pier and a natural reef less than a mile offshore, waves have been constructively redirected toward shore, often forming bigger and consistently better quality breakers to surf.

When the Sheboygan surfers decided to create an identification system, they began naming all of the various breaks based on their location. With an eye toward finding those ideal surf breaks on his own, Larry first came upon three or four near the C. Reiss Coal Company on Sheboygan's south side. Since the 1880s, the site served as a storage and distribution facility for coal, rock salt, and petroleum products that skirted out toward the water's edge. Because the company prohibited pedestrians on that portion of the beach, it created the ideal surfing sanctuary for anyone seeking privacy on his board. As the little Pomeranian dog and Larry scampered along the Northside Pier, they came upon one of the biggest and best breaks on the Great Lakes, the bend in the pier known as the Elbow. Over the next few years, all of the breaks would receive nicknames, usually based on their location among the city-installed ladders and jetties along the pier. Beyond the first jetty, second jetty, and third jetty was the fourth, or "broken" jetty, a heap of concrete rubble twisted by Lake Michigan's harsh winter waves. Then there was a large limestone outcropping known as the Niagara Escarpment, which some consider the Mount Everest of freshwater surfing because of its three distinctive breaks. If the waves got really big, the surfers would go out to the seventeenth ladder.

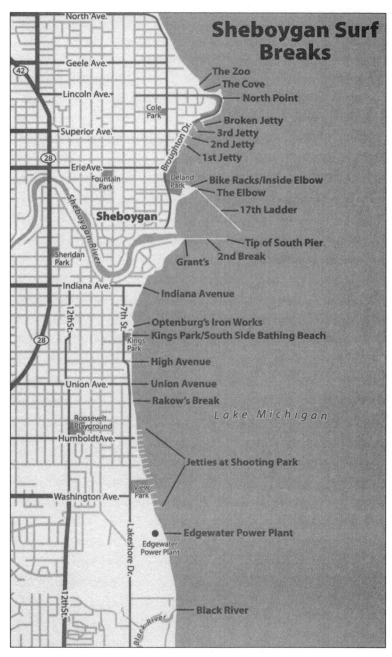

MAP CREATED BY CLERISY PRESS

Around the corner from the pier was North Point, a cove that wrapped calm waters around the leeward side, majestically peeling off into the cove. Under the right conditions, which occurred only once or twice a year, the waves climbed the city's retaining wall, resurging the same size wave going out. When that wave met an oncoming wave, a five- or six-foot plume of water would burst just about anybody off his board, sending even the best surfer ten feet in the air. It was all part of the excitement and unpredictability of surfing North Point.

Just north was a break known as the Zoo. It was located on the banks of the Sheboygan Zoo, which at most housed twenty animals. Surfers accessed the water through a service road behind a high chain-link fence that, rumor had it, enclosed one of the meanest bison east of the Mississippi River. Rumor or not, Larry's little Pomeranian insisted on walking as far away from the fence as possible. The dog's sense of fear did little to dissuade Larry's giddiness about his discoveries that morning. As quickly as he could, he raced home to tell his brother about the little corner of the world they'd be able to visit all on their own.

For the next three years, Lee and Larry measured the quality of their previous day's beach experience by how much sand they found in their bed the next morning. If they found nothing, the previous day wasn't a good one.

Growing up on Sheboygan's less privileged south side, Lee and Larry often had little money, and hanging at the beach was the cheapest entertainment in town. Even when ice and snow blanketed the sand, Lee and Larry braved the harshest weather conditions to enjoy the free fun from sunup to sundown. In summer they splashed in one of the world's largest swimming pools, and in winter one of the world's largest ice-skating rinks was just a couple blocks from their house.

Conversations at the Williams' dinner table frequently concerned Lee and Larry's growing fascination with the beach. Jack
Williams, having grown up on the water, promoted their passion.
Mom, on the other hand, couldn't swim a stroke and struggled to
comprehend the whole surfing craze and beach lifestyle that was
sweeping the country. Fearing the unknown, she forbade them
from stepping into the water when there was the slightest chance
of snow or accumulated crust of ice on the edge of the lake—end
of conversation. The boys countered her policy with cloak and
dagger resistance.

One Easter weekend when they were thirteen, Mary and Jack
Williams crashed out for a Sunday afternoon nap. Downstairs
in the basement, Lee and Larry plotted to meet their friends,
who were surfing in seasonably slushy waters. Putting on their
wetsuits underneath their clothes, the boys opened the basement window as quietly as possible in hope of sneaking out. But
the hinges creaked loud enough to cause the dogs to bark three
doors down. Only their father's chainsaw snoring masked their
getaway as they slid their board out in front of them. Clear of
any immediate obstructions, Lee and Larry headed for the water,
not even considering how they'd sneak back into the house later.
They thought only of catching a couple of waves. Without boots,
gloves, or hoods, they wouldn't last much longer than a couple
of waves in the frigid Lake Michigan waters.

Upon arriving at the beach, Lee and Larry counted only a
few brave souls in the water. Around the bonfire, which had been
roaring on the shore long enough to melt a ring of sand between
the flames and snow-covered beach, stood a handful of Easter
Day surfers from the Great Lakes Surf Club. The fire's glowing
embers did little to comfort those who had already wiped out
in the chilled waters. From the look of the waves, they'd gotten
hit just as the impact of the water tore the board out from under
them. Without ankle leashes, the wipeout victims—freezing hair

and all—had to retrieve their lost boards, often swimming all the way back to shore. It was a guarantee to end one's day prematurely, left to shiver, hoping to regain feeling in otherwise numb extremities. The club members congregated around the bonfire didn't even flinch when their legs began steaming, a surefire sign the cold water encapsulating them was leaving their bodies. Even when somebody warmed up, the odds of summoning enough courage to go back out were slim. Those left to sulk around the bonfire spitefully watched the water, cheering for other wipeout victims to join them.

Still, it seemed as soon as someone set down a surfboard—because there weren't that many around—somebody else would grab it, braving the conditions in a never-ending spiral of one-upmanship. The excitement often led those who had already wiped out to laugh lake water out of their noses when the next guy took an even bigger digger, prematurely ending his wave ride with an ungraceful face-plant. As soon as he rocketed out of the water, a blood-curdling scream that could be heard as far away as Door County preceded his panic-stricken scramble for shore.

None of that fazed Lee and Larry as they walked past the bonfire and stepped into the water. To them, there was something almost religious about surfing. It was freedom that drove them, something they couldn't explain or experience in other places. "I'm just glad our little slice of heaven is only a few blocks from home," Lee said as he awaited his first wave in waist-deep water.

Paddling through the shore break, they made it past the lull before reaching a second, more intimidating shore break with massive barrels that continually pounded down in the impact zone. "We'll definitely be doing seventy percent swimming and thirty percent surfing," Larry said. "But that's what surfing on Lake Mi—"

With the force of a kitchen stove being dropped on his face, a distracted Larry was thrown off his board by a series of waves, nearly knocking him silly. Calculating that just one gallon of water weighs 8.34 pounds, it must have seemed like nearly two tons of water had thrashed him around like a washing machine. Propelled head-over-heels into a belly flop that skipped him across the water like a stone, Larry was shaken until he finally bounced off the bottom. Regaining his senses, he popped up to the surface while readjusting the broken seams on his wetsuit.

"Whoa," he roared. "I can't believe I lived through that!" Shaking his head a few times to recover his senses, he grabbed his board and paddled out again.

Just as he was about to turn around to challenge another wave, he saw Mary and Jack Williams standing on the shoreline, obviously awake from their nap. Dad was grinning ear to ear, knowing his boys had been caught in the act. Mom looked far less pleased.

"Are you crazy?" she yelled. "There's still ice on the lake!"

"It's warm, Mom," Larry said as he walked to shore. "You can't believe how warm we are in here."

Unconvinced, Mary demanded Larry unzip his wetsuit. When she was about to place her hand inside, steam billowed out, proving he wasn't lying. What she didn't realize was that the five-millimeter layer of neoprene separating Larry's skin from the water was the result of a fellow surfer's recent engineering phenomenon.

Prior to 1952, there weren't a whole lot of options for water-sports enthusiasts to combat the cold. Several grand experiments with bulky canvas jumpers and World War II flight suits had not really worked. Finally Jack O'Neill, a hardcore surfer in northern California, stitched together a suit of synthetic rubber, called neoprene, so he could continue riding waves when the water started getting cold. As Mary learned that afternoon, the suits didn't work by keeping the surfer dry, but rather by letting the water in and having the surfer's body heat warm it inside the suit. From that day forward, Lee and Larry had their mother's blessing to push the limits of surfing in even colder water, surrounded by even bigger icebergs, engaging even bigger waves.

Although she never truly understood it, Mary tried to take an interest in her sons' growing passion, often asking what the adrenaline rush felt like. "Not everyone can do it," Larry told her. "It's like walking a tightrope on a windy day where there's just that little window of when you're riding the wave and having the courage to do it. With the goal being just over that next wave, you're spinning that surfboard around as fast as you can and paddling hard to catch that wave to get the rush, regardless if it's two feet or ten."

She looked at him with a motherly mix of interest and concern.

Lee stepped in. "Once you make it out there and you sit up on your board like you're sitting on a kitchen chair, you don't even think about the wiggles, the waggles, the chop, the wind. To get covered up or get a little head dip on a two-footer when you're on the nose can be as big a rush as dropping down a ten-foot face and you're just inches away from being eaten alive by that wave. Then you look around and the people in the lineup are your best friends. That's what it's all about, Mom."

Mom nodded, understanding a little bit better now but still unsure.

That spring after their first winter of surfing, the Williams brothers were willing to do whatever it took to encourage the seasonal surf to arrive as quickly as possible. Applying what they had learned during the school year about Roman mythology, they decided to make Neptune, the god of water, an offering. So on a brisk Saturday evening, Lee, Larry, Kevin, Rich Kuitert, and Jeff Schultz built a bonfire on the beach. They filled an empty five-gallon paint bucket with lake water, beach grass, urine, dead alewife fish, a used condom they found on the sand, and an old rusty bed spring to signify their appreciation for waves. Within moments, the burning stench filled the air, nearly gagging them. Only a teenager focused on tempting the surf gods could tolerate the burning in his eyes and nausea percolating in his stomach. Caught up in the moment, the young surfers danced around their boiling kettle of stink, chanting made-up words as they raised driftwood spears into the air. Their offensive concoction of solemn-o-juice drew more attention from lakefront residents living downwind than it drew from the surf gods, but enough waves arrived the following weekend for the boys to feel their tribal ceremony had made a difference, justifying future offerings in the years to come.

As the snowdrifts melted, blossoms filled the cherry trees and dandelions popped up even in the most manicured lawns. The signs of spring signaled summer's approach. While most fathers of middle-school boys marked the season by breaking in a new baseball glove or by spending a Saturday afternoon restocking a fishing tackle box, Jack Williams was left smelling the unmistakable aroma of burning wax emanating from the family kitchen.

Hosting their very own impromptu wax party with friends, Lee and Larry put the solid paraffin wax bars into emptied five-pound coffee cans, which then were placed over the stove to boil into liquid. The wax, often used for canning, smelled nothing like the scented coconut versions available in later years, and the odor lingered for days. The technique of waxing surfboards to increase traction for feet and hands had been around since at least the early 1900s, when candle droppings were wiped to a clean sheen with a cloth.

Once the wax had melted, the boys poured the liquid concoction onto their boards. They waxed the boards outside for obvious reasons. It was like dousing gasoline onto a new lawn and often resulted in a perfect white outline of a surfboard where all the wax had melted into the grass.

Taking their newly waxed board to the beach, Lee and Larry would rub sand in the glossy wax to make it more abrasive and grip-able. Although this was the trendy thing to do, the sand on the board's surface rubbed against their skin like sandpaper, often chewing big holes through their wetsuits. Rubbing knees and toes raw, the technique left behind what are affectionately called surfer knots. Before the open wounds hardened into calluses, they often got infected from the dirty storm water and big surf churning up sediment off the lake bottom. The infections did little to deter Lee and Larry. Though swollen and sore, they were often back surfing two or three days later with a new wax job on their board.

Lee graduated from Farnsworth Junior High School that spring. Larry was held back a year in the fifth grade for what he cited as, "The teachers thinking I was so intelligent, they chose to keep me around for another year to see what else they could learn." With the warmer weather, their focus returned to the Great Lakes Surf Club. They were no longer rookies, but rather a group of boys eager to be more daring with their surfing excursions.

Although surfing off Sheboygan's coal yards didn't have the glamour of Australia's Gold Coast or San Diego's La Jolla Shores, the boys remained as committed as ever. During the winter they had upgraded to brand new Wardy surfboards. Mail ordered from California at the cost of one hundred and fifty dollars plus an extra twenty-five for shipping, the boards were heavy, weighing nearly fifty pounds each. They were quite the behemoths for the brothers, who weighed in the neighborhood of seventy-five pounds apiece. On more than one occasion while in transit from the beach, the boards tipped off the heads of their transporters onto the concrete sidewalk, but never once did they chip or show any signs of damage. Their durability guaranteed that Lee and Larry would have no problem recouping their investment by surfing unmercifully on Lake Michigan that summer. The boards' invincibility fueled the boys' sense of immortality as they continually dared one another in outrageous challenges of one-upmanship.

With Kevin Groh in tow that first weekend of summer vacation in 1967, the Williams brothers, with freshly waxed surfboards in hand, stood alongside the banks of the Sheboygan River. Looking at the water that divided the city—physically, sociologically, and financially—they were all too familiar with this forced detour in their daily pilgrimage between their house on the south side and their favorite surf breaks to the north.

On a dare born out of frustration, birthed from constantly having to route themselves over two miles to cross the river on the Eighth Street bridge, the three boys stared across the river at the US Coast Guard station. Aware that the closely guarded channel was too dangerous to accommodate any sort of pedestrian traffic with ore carriers, sailboats, fishing vessels, and a wicked current, they measured up the two hundred yards in front of them. "Well, who's gonna put their board in first?" Kevin challenged.

Lee and Larry looked at each other and then back at Kevin—a daring gaze, which was immediately returned. They all threw their surfboards into the river.

"Last one to the other side is a valley cowboy," Lee yelled, knowing nobody wanted to be labeled as an inland surfer. That was an insult worse than "gremmie" or "dork" or "hodad."

As soon as the Coast Guard officer on duty saw the surfboards splash into the river, he sounded the emergency claxon and bellowed into the PA system, "There are bodies in the navigation channel!"

With the emergency sirens blaring, a Coast Guard cutter jetted out of the Sheboygan Harbor toward the paddling trio with the specific instructions, "Get those people out of the water, now!"

Treating the claxon as a starting gun, the boys raced across the harbor, with the ultimate prize being to not get arrested. Unbeknownst to them, the harbor was hosting a sailboat race that day. The same waves on the lake that motivated Lee, Larry, and Kevin to surf on the north side of town that morning were too big to safely host boats dependent on wind. Once the first sailboat silently passed their waterlogged noggins, the boys' paddling went from a steady hustle to avoid the Coast Guard to a frantic flailing in hopes of keeping their heads, literally.

The lightning-class sailboats whizzed across the waters completely unaware of the boys. When the spectators and boat skippers began to notice the human buoys bobbing in the water on their boards, they shouted at them, "Get out before you get yourselves killed!"

But the scolding and yelling only strengthened the boys' resolve to disrupt the afternoon's status quo. It was no longer a daring race between friends, but rather a test to see if three teenagers could out-swim, outmaneuver, and outsmart a Coast Guard cutter in hot pursuit without getting sliced apart by an oncoming sailboat—all while making it to the other side first.

The boys reached the shore within strokes of one another, navigating the choppy water and landing on the riverbank's north side before the Coast Guard cutter or any race official could catch up. Now on foot, the three disappeared into the labyrinth of alleyways behind the town's main street shops. Although a police dragnet would have most likely found them, Sheboygan didn't have enough law enforcement personnel to go chasing thrill-seeking teenagers. Lee, Larry, and Kevin had pulled off their stunt and fulfilled the surfers' mantra of pushing the limits at any cost.

Word soon traveled throughout Sheboygan's surfing circles of their race across the river, earning them instant street credibility. Although it didn't generate an invitation into the Lake Shore Surf

Club, the incident did give them confidence and a reason to feel more accepted among their peers.

A few weeks later, Larry was heading to the beach to meet up with the Great Lakes Surfing Club members. After passing the Optenberg's Ironworks factory with a skimboard under his arm, he noticed Andy Sommersberger's red and white Dodge van approaching. Larry expected to be ignored despite wearing a Hawaiian shirt decorated with surfboards and a pair of tattered cutoffs. Instead, as he drove by, Andy gave a modest wave. Larry was stunned—and elated. He finally received the sliver of acknowledgement he had craved for nearly two years. He spent the rest of his trek to the sand in a haze, eager to tell the others but in some ways wanting to savor the moment all by himself.

Chapter Three

During one of the last days of summer vacation that year, Larry and Lee's kook board mysteriously disappeared. Since they lived in Sheboygan, a town where theft was practically non-existent, especially of a surfboard, the list of suspects was short. No APBs blared across the police radio band. No warrants were issued to search residential homes. And no private detectives were hired to solve "the case of the missing surfboard."

For weeks, rumors of the board's whereabouts persisted— some serious, some nothing more than snickering wisecracks. It wasn't surprising that the suspects were a group of upperclassmen on the eve of their senior year looking to reestablish their age dominance over the young surfers. As the Great Lake Surf Club's elder statesmen, Lee and Larry decided to bide their time, knowing a one-hundred-pound cigar box couldn't inconspicuously hide in Sheboygan forever.

Their investigation led them to the beach, specifically the city lifeguard station. There, perched behind the counter, along with three members of the Lake Shore Surf Club, was the surfboard. "We'll take OUR surfboard back now!" Larry said sternly.

The biggest of the three adversaries took a long drag from his cigarette, puffed out his chest in a show of defiance, and replied in a low monotone: "No."

Then followed a quick exchange of four-letter insults that only teenagers could decipher. Lee, tired of arguing, walked behind the counter and yanked the board out of the grasp of the stoutest of the three without saying a word. Never short of pleasantries, Lee politely obliged with, "Thank you."

The gunfire of insults silenced into wicked glares. With board in hand, Lee and Larry walked out of the lifeguard station. Not a fist was raised in solving "the case of the missing surfboard."

Once word spread around school of how the Williams twins commandeered their surfboard back from the seniors, it seemed that everybody tried to test Larry's volatile temper. Not a week went by when he wasn't involved in a pushing or shouting match, often including a few flying fists or somebody getting driven into the ground gripped in a headlock.

Tired of being sassed and harassed, Larry decided to make an example out of a foulmouthed runt two years his junior during one of the Great Lakes Surf Club's weekend surfing excursions. After ignoring nearly two hours of insults and innuendos that would make a Las Vegas prostitute blush, Larry buried the loud-mouth up to his neck in sand. Knowing the brat was unable to move, he proceeded to drop a big rotting fish on his head, leaving him there to bake in the sun.

For the next hour, the brat struggled to wiggle himself free—to no avail. A passing police officer realized he was the victim and not a willing participant in a prank, and after fifteen minutes of digging, the officer exhumed the kid from the sandy grave. But the smell of dead carp would linger in his hair for days, reminding him of his place on the surfers' hierarchy.

Despite their growing confidence, Lee and Larry were still taken aback when Rocky Groh insinuated to them that the Lake Shore Surf Club was getting together for a little holiday debauchery at the local Pizza Hut. They interpreted the hint as an unofficial invitation to join them that night, knowing it was conditional.

"If the three of you sit quietly at a separate table and don't cause any trouble," Rocky said, "we won't shove you away. But one squeal out of your corner and we'll bounce you out of there higher than a SuperBall."

Although offered in passing by one of Andy Sommersberger's lieutenants, the invite was monumental on several levels. For the past two years, the Lake Shore Surf Club members had been the kings of the Sheboygan surf scene with Lee, Larry, Kevin, and the handful of other Great Lakes Surf Club members serving in their loyal court as silent observers. Not only was it the first time the Lake Shore Surf Club extended any sort of courtesies to the younger generation of surfers, but never before had the group included anybody outside of their tight clique to join them, in any capacity, for any function of any kind. If the boys had been offered the invitation while surfing, their excitement might have allowed them to walk across the waves without getting their toenails wet.

That night, as soon as their shift of washing dishes and bussing tables at Geno's Top of the First ended, they raced to Pizza Hut. It was Christmas season, so the restaurant was packed with dozens of college students home on break with their families. Right in the middle of the restaurant five tables had been pulled together to form one master table with at least thirteen guys from the Lake Shore Surf Club sitting among the pizzas and sodas and beers.

All of the Lake Shore Surf Club regulars were there, and from the way they guzzled pitcher after pitcher after pitcher, they seemed to have just returned from a desert retreat. At the head of the table, Randy Grimmer shoved a whole slice of pizza into his mouth while still carrying on a conversation with Mark Hall and Bill Kuitert. Cheering Randy on was Johnny Rusch, who looked more like an accountant than a surfer. It would have seemed like the club kept him around to keep up their grade point average, if they had been recognized by the high school as a legitimate organization. He mostly served as the target of their teasing, often receiving atomic-wedgies, where the back of his underwear was pulled over the front of his face. Everyone knew when he got one, as his bow-legged gait through the high school hallways was a dead giveaway. But tonight, he was a part of the festivities and sat right in the middle of the drinking and eating.

At the other end of the table, Rocky Groh showcased his ability to eat pizza and drink beer while keeping his unfiltered Camel cigarette balanced on his lips. When he noticed Kevin, Lee, and Larry's arrival, he gave them only a slight glance implying, "Don't make me look bad." Tom Ziegler and Andy Sommersberger sat at the opposite end of the table from where Genyk Okolowicz chimed in on sing-alongs whenever the verse struck him, adding to the already obnoxious scene created by the group. Although never acknowledged amid the hooting and hollering, an awkward silence occasionally fell on the table. Those brief moments of silence were reminders that the night's dinner was the last hurrah for several of those guys before being forced to face adulthood. Some were only a few months from high school graduation, and the Vietnam War loomed in their minds. At eighteen, they didn't want to be forced to pick up a gun and shoot people halfway across the world.

Some tried for college deferment. Others faked illnesses. Andy Sommersberger, in typical fashion, went to another extreme. Remembering Rocky's rash from earlier in the summer, he had soaked his wetsuit in gasoline a month before having to go down for his entrance physical. On the day before his entrance exam, he slipped into the petroleum-soaked suit. As gasoline seeped into his pores, the eye-watering sensation intensified. Convinced that pain is weakness leaving the body, Andy kept reminding himself it was all worth the price he was paying. No amount of burning, itching, or nausea compared to the months of hell ahead of him if he couldn't scheme his way out of Southeast Asia. He wasn't a soldier; he was a surfer, and failure on this mission was not an option unless he wanted to exchange his board for a rifle.

The next day an ecstatic Andy Sommersberger exited the US Army Examination and Entrance Station. Uncle Sam had issued him a medical deferment. All thirteen of the Lake Shore Surf Club members, despite being of draft age, avoided serving a day in camouflage fatigues through one means or another.

Maybe Andy's recent victory over Uncle Sam was cause for such loud and brash behavior at the Pizza Hut that night. As the group's leader, he set the tone for the whole evening. Since he was smiling and laughing that night, the rest of the table was throwing food and making obnoxious noises with various appendages. Quietly sitting in a corner booth, Kevin, Lee, and Larry just observed.

The group's shenanigans went on for quite a while until the restaurant got very quiet. At first, the boys continued their conversation, not paying any attention to the rest of the patrons. They figured Andy and the gang were having a moment of reflection, until. . . .

"Son of a bitch," screamed an angry waitress. She slung four-letter words while slashing at the empty cups, plates, and napkins on the table. Customers at the other tables stared in wonder. That's when Kevin noticed: "They dashed without paying the bill."

"Amazing," Larry said with a smile. "They can turn an average pizza- and-beer night into a chance to push the limits."

Lee nodded, though he clearly was less impressed.

"Aren't they great?" Larry said.

"It sure is typical of those guys," Lee answered.

Lee and Larry began getting invited to hang out in the water just on the outskirts of where many of the Lake Shore Surf Club members rode the waves. As the youngest of the group, they were still trying to impress. They tried to be as stylish and outrageous as possible. But when they looked down the beach and saw a couple of kids riding in waves on a break just south of them, they couldn't help but feel as if their thunder had been stolen—especially when Andy, Rocky, Randy, and the rest of the older boys noticed.

"Who are those guys?" Andy asked his gang. "Anybody ever seen those boards before?"

"I think they're from Black River," Randy said. "I heard a couple of guys are surfing there now."

"What a bunch of kooks," Rocky chimed in. "Probably driving in every day from Fond du Lac."

For the next few weeks it seemed every time the Sheboygan surfers hit the water, those two guys from Black River were paddling out and riding in with them wave for wave just to the south. Proving they weren't one-wave wonders, the two freelance riders began earning the respect of the Sheboygan surfers. So when the "Black River surfing rats"—as they were nicknamed by several of the Lake Shore Surf Clubbers—decided to wander north, Lee and Larry introduced themselves on behalf of the group.

Even the most cliché of surfing jargon seemed fresh when the Williams brothers began chatting up the Black River surfing rats—Mark Rakow and Mark Wente. Since all four were about the same age, it didn't take long for them to bond over the adage, "You really can't have a bad day at the beach." After about twenty minutes, when all four decided they were wasting the opportunity to ride some good waves by standing on the sand, they began shoving their surfboards into the water. For the next couple of hours, the four boys took turns on the crest of a wave, hotdogging, gliding, and inhaling the freedom of the surf.

Since most of the Lake Shore Surf Club members were on the verge of graduation, the Great Lakes Surf Club continued to attract new members their age. As the weather got nicer in the spring of 1968, parties at the beach became more prevalent. Even

with the increased foot traffic on the sand, it still wasn't
busy enough to scare away
foxes, coyotes, and all sorts
of birds. The Lake Shore
Surf Club's favorite spot
for hosting hooters was a
cove near the C. Reiss Coal
Company on Sheboygan's
south side. It was so hidden
nobody could see what was
going on from the road or
anywhere else on the beach
unless they were right on
top of the outcropping.
Even when the police drove

The sun shines on Larry and his board.

by, they didn't bother to get out of their squad cars to patrol the
area, knowing that as long as everyone was tucked away from
sight, the situation didn't require their attention.

"You could walk around naked and nobody would know," Lee
often joked. Thanks to the magical mix of alcohol and young people, several of the partygoers did eventually walk around the cove
naked, much to the enjoyment of everybody who was there.

Eager to learn anything about the surfing lifestyle, Lee and
Larry picked up whatever they could find regarding the Hawaiian
and Californian surf scenes, while incorporating their unique
Sheboygan flavor. If there was a decal, a sticker, or a t-shirt they
could get their hands on, they made sure everybody within the
Great Lakes Surf Club had the chance to buy one. As the school
year transitioned into summer vacation in 1968, their little en-
trepreneurship wasn't necessarily turning a profit, but it wasn't
breaking them either.

The 1968 Lake Shore Surf Club poses in front of the Sheboygan County Court House. Present for this photo: Chuck Reis, Tyler Cooper, Mark Rakow, Bill Kuitert, Tom Grabielse, Jim Schmidt, Chuck Koehler, Jeff Sherman, Rocky Groh, Ron Wilke, Rich Kuitert, Al Kuitert, Mark Wente, Mark Hall, Don Wilds, Andy Sommersberger, Tom Ziegler, Larry Williams, Lee Williams, Kevin Groh, Larry Sommersberger, and Randy Grimmer

Their success did garner an invitation that summer to participate in one of the earliest group photos of any surfing organization in the history of the Great Lakes. Standing on the stairs of the Sheboygan County Courthouse, front and center were Lee and Larry Williams with twenty-three of their fellow surfers, including Kevin Groh, Mark Rakow, Mark Wente, and Chuck Koehler standing alongside Lake Shore Surf Club members Bill Kuitert, Rocky Groh, Randy Grimmer, Mark Hall, Tom Ziegler, and Andy Sommersberger. The photo captured the magnitude of the Sheboygan surfing scene that summer, successfully bringing together both generations of surfers before events outside of anyone's control would alter many of their lives forever.

For the Lake Shore Surf Club, the photograph signified the last time they gathered as a group since the reality of adulthood had reared its ugly head only a few months earlier. On Friday night, February 16, 1968, Lake Shore Surf Club members Genyk Okolowicz and Andy Sommersberger met up with classmates Bill Karl and Craig Schwalenberg, who drove them from bar to bar on dirt-covered Sheboygan County roads.

In a scene right out of Animal House, they pulled into the dusty parking lot of an old, three-story, Victorian, beat-up-piece-of-crap of a tavern known prophetically as "The Bitter End." Within moments of their arrival, a gorgeous woman rushed up to Genyk's friend Johnny Rusch, who was far from being a lady's man with his collared polo shirt and color-coordinated shorts. His favorite line when trying to pick up a date, which often resulted in rolled eyes or a slap in the face, was "Nice legs. Are those rentals?"

So when she propositioned him with a seductive, "Let's go out to your car and make love," Genyk, never one to interfere with another's attempt at finding happiness inside someone's pants, wished his friend well and struck up a conversation with a group of friends next to him.

Johnny chugged the last of his beer and slammed the empty mug onto the bar quoting Kaiser Wilhelm, "Give me a woman who loves beer and I will conquer the world!"

Eagerly following the mysterious buxom blonde out the door and across the parking lot, Johnny navigated the maze of treacherous tire ruts and tree root knots, knowing his window of opportunity would slam shut if he wiped out. Thanks to his strong sense of balance from endless hours on surfboards atop Lake Michigan waves, he was soon sprawled in the backseat of a Pontiac Tempest.

Sparked by her hypnotic seduction, he tore off his clothes in less than a minute. Just when she reached down to unbutton her blouse, a couple of country thugs in denim swung open the car door. She winked at him and hopped out as the burliest goon grabbed Johnny's pants, wallet, and everything that had been on his person in one quick motion. Before Johnny could surmise what had happened, the girl and two guys had run off into the woods. There he was left in his birthday suit with nothing to show for his backseat tryst other than a bruised ego.

"I've been raped," a stark-naked Johnny cried as he stormed into the packed bar. "Help me. Two thugs just stole everything."

"Except your dignity," heckled a girl from the back of the bar. "But you lost that when you ran in here." When the crowd laughed, Johnny broke into tears. A sympathetic bartender draped him in a tablecloth and escorted him to a back room away from the snickering crowd. A few hours later, while riding home in the backseat of a police cruiser, it dawned on him that his embarrassment would be the talk of the town. "I should've known she was a setup," he later told friends. "Honestly, who giggles at a quote from the German Emperor who lost World War I before getting laid?"

Back in the bar, Craig, Genyk, Bill, and Andy were the life of the party. Ordering shots all-around before hitting the road, they soon found themselves stumbling down the deteriorating Victorian stairs and across the hardened tire ruts without even an ounce of grace. Once behind the wheel, Craig tried his best to navigate down the unlit, two-lane county road.

One thing led to another—and the jeep flipped.

When Bill and Andy came to their senses, all they could hear was the jeep's twisted metal groaning like the final cry of some wounded beast. Wiping dried blood from underneath his nostril, Andy noticed a faint smell of smoke and oil hanging in the air. Covered in slivers of glass from the windshield, they looked around and saw how far they had been tossed from the crashed vehicle. At first, all they could make out was the jeep's front end crumpled into the front seat with both the steering wheel and dashboard compacted into one mangled mess. Getting to their feet and staggering to the mangled mess, they saw that the passenger door was torn free from its hinges and its two front-seat passengers unaccounted for. After that, all was silent for a while.

Craig was jettisoned from the vehicle and killed instantly. Ten yards from the overturned jeep, Genyk lay on the side of the road and would die a day later from his injuries. It was the first time anybody from the Lake Shore Surf Club had to look death directly in the face. For Bill and Andy, it was bleeding in their arms at the bottom of a ditch.

Weeks passed but the horror and grief over Genyk and Craig's deaths seemed to grow rather than fade. Any attempts at trying to "turn back the clock to the way it was" before the incident failed miserably. Andy Sommersberger, Tom Ziegler, Randy Grimmer, Rocky Groh, and the rest of the Lake Shore Surf Club were forced to re-examine the purpose of their lives. As eighteen- year-olds on the verge of adulthood, life had slapped them upside the head with a cold case of reality.

The reverberations went well beyond the universe of fourteen-year-old surfers, most of whom weren't old enough to know Genyk like the Lake Shore Surf Club guys did. They could, however, see from a distance how his death shook the entire Sheboygan community, especially their surfing idols.

Over the course of the summer, the Lake Shore Surf Club began to quietly dissolve as members drifted away to begin their futures. Some guys got married; some left for college; others just disappeared after successfully dodging the draft. Although there was no formal announcement or specific moment when it was decided the group was disbanding, by Labor Day of 1968, the Lake Shore Surf Club was becoming a topic spoken of only in the past tense. The Sheboygan surfing legacy was now left in the hands of the Williams brothers and the Great Lakes Surf Club.

Second Wave

Chapter Four

During the last few months of 1968, the Sheboygan surfing scene found itself in a state of flux following the tragic deaths of Genyk Okolowicz and Craig Schwalenberg. Only a few brave souls found the passion necessary to withstand the harsh conditions of frigid Lake Michigan with a board that winter. Although deeply affected by Genyk's death, the Williams brothers were eager to revive the stagnant Sheboygan surf scene. As part of the area's younger surf regime, their destiny wasn't tied to the older generation's fate. Instead, they found themselves with the tools to begin carving a new chapter into Sheboygan's burgeoning surf history. But they were burdened that winter with weather that would not cooperate with their wave-riding aspirations.

While stories about tourists disappearing, only to be found again during Sheboygan's spring thaw of 1969, were rife in Sun Belt newspapers, Lake Michigan's uninspiring surfing conditions didn't attract even a drop of ink. Unable to appreciate the flowers blossoming, grass turning green, or robins nesting in nearby trees, Lee and Larry were left frustrated and bored. Since school was always an afterthought behind surfing and their part-time jobs, they struggled to find legitimate activities to keep themselves occupied.

Lake Michigan was inhospitable to surfers, leaving the Williams twins with no outlet for their rambunctious instincts. Their

Larry surfing North Point

boredom soon found relief at the Pool Tavern, a local watering hole at the corner of downtown Sheboygan's Indiana Avenue and Ninth Street, just six snowdrift-covered blocks from their home. Thanks to the kindness of its owner, Joe Udovich, the kids were invited to hang out in the bar's basement. As a strong Christian, Joe wanted to provide the neighborhood youngsters with a safe place to socialize by offering inexpensive sodas, lunch items, and games such as pool and darts. Little did Joe realize he would be hosting such a collection of hellions!

The teenagers spent their first days in the basement playing eight ball, pinball, and cricket. When that got boring, they started roughhousing, which led to a few broken drink glasses and cracked pool balls. The forgiving owner looked at it as nothing more than anticipated collateral damage from a group of teenagers. However, when the boys continued their destruction, Joe reluctantly installed a security camera in the basement, allowing the bartender upstairs to monitor their actions at all times.

As expected, the eye in the sky only prompted the boys to figure out which corners of the room were and weren't monitored upstairs. At first they tested the peripheral vision of the camera by making faces into the lens. When that didn't elicit a response from the aloof bartenders upstairs—most of whom weren't interested in becoming a babysitting service, at least to sober teenagers who were too cheap to tip—the entire group of boys unleashed *Lord of the Flies*-style testosterone-driven dares.

At first the dares were innocent. Jeff Schultz stacked whisky tumblers into elaborate three-dimensional pyramids. Rich Kuitert shot spitballs from across the room towards the camera. Then, Kevin and Rocky Groh broke cue sticks over each other's heads when dueling with them as if they were medieval swords. When Larry brought down his BB gun, everybody thought he was going to show it off by shooting at some paper, cardboard, or tin can targets. Ignoring the warning on the box to "be sure to provide adult supervision until you've instilled good gun safety rules in the child," Larry loaded hatpins into it and started firing them at the dartboard. Thinking the gun was empty, he aimed it across the room at Lee, who was ignoring his brother's antics in hopes of hitting his next pool shot.

Thweet! The punctured hatpin stuck all the way into Lee's leg, with only the blue ball on the end exposed outside the skin.

"I didn't think it was loaded," Larry said, apologizing profusely.

Realizing Lee was furious, Larry dropped the gun and fled for the door.

Without breaking eye contact with his brother, not even to blink, Lee picked up the cue ball, hurling it at him with the velocity of a Nolan Ryan fastball. Larry ducked, and the sound of the ball striking him in the back of the skull delivered a wallop to the guts of every boy in the room. Larry lay motionless as the ricocheted cue ball bounced back onto his groin.

The room fell dead silent. They could hear the chatter of the bar patrons above them, the rattling of glasses, the thump of footsteps. But downstairs—nothing. Not a sound. Coming to his senses, Larry rubbed the orange-sized lump on the back of his skull.

"Are we even now?" he asked.

"Sure," Lee said, relieved that he'd not killed his brother, even as he pried the hatpin from his calf.

A few weeks later, Lee walked into the wood-paneled basement with what looked like a stick of dynamite in hand, exclaiming, "It's Fourth of July in February!"

"Are you nuts?" Larry said. "You're going to burn the place down."

"It's just a railroad flare. They're harmless."

After making sure he was out of range of the camera, Lee ignited it.

"Let's light this party up," he said. Once the flare was lit, smoke poured out of it.

"Blow it out! They're going to see it on the camera," Rich said.

"We can't afford to get busted," Jeff said. "We have nowhere else to go."

"Throw it in the toilet," Larry told his brother. He ran toward the bathroom door.

Since teenage boys don't often think through potential consequences before taking action, Lee followed his brother completely on instinct. He figured that water extinguishes fire so putting the burning wick of a flare into a bowl of water should take care of this smoke problem.

Racing into the bathroom holding the flare high and proud like the Olympic torch, Lee stepped up to the bowl of cool water with the plume of thick smoke trailing him. His group of apostles behind him watched every move. He tossed the stick into the toilet water, awaiting the soothing hiss of an extinguished wick.

He didn't hear it.

"What the hell," he said. "Why's it still burning?"

The wick continued to burn towards the flare's shaft as a fury of bubbles frothed over the edges of the porcelain bowl. The group of curious onlookers wrestled one another for a prime viewing position to the impending train wreck. "Let me see," they bickered. "Why's it still burning underwater?" one inquired.

With the wick burned down almost to the shaft's nub, the reality of the impending outcome set in. "We gotta get out of here!" Rocky warned as the boys tumbled out of the bathroom. "That's gonna explode like a bomb!"

Just as the last hooligan fled the bathroom, a muffled implosion rocketed a plume of water out of the stall, splashing water on the musty, grouted tile floor. Curious to see the results of their mischief, Lee and a handful of followers raced back into the bathroom, only to be met by a gushing wall of water.

"The toilet cracked! We broke the bowl," Lee yelled as toilet water rushed across the basement floor.

They all stood in horror, wondering what to do.

"We have to act natural so nobody knows we messed up down here," Rocky offered. With the water level threatening to rise above the soles of their Chuck Taylor high-tops, the boys headed up the stairs as nonchalantly as possible to avoid bringing attention to their toilet-soaked shenanigans. If only the bartender on shift cared enough to question why the boys' shoes made that squishing sound as they walked out the door, Pool Tavern owner Joe Udovich would have had a lead in solving "The Case of the Cracked Toilet." Instead, he was left without a clue.

For Lee and Larry, practical jokes were a way of life. At an early age, they witnessed their mother enforcing family rules through what might kindly be called practical jokes—none more memorable than when their father came home drunk one night from the local bar, Benjie's. Toasted from a night of heavy drinking, Jack Williams plopped himself down at the kitchen table hoping the room would stop spinning. When he sneezed, his dentures flew straight across the room. Oblivious that he had lost his teeth, Jack proceeded to wipe his nose before sauntering upstairs for the night. Thoroughly frustrated with his behavior, Mary walked to the corner of the kitchen and picked up the dentures. Wrapping them in a handkerchief, she stored them away.

The next morning when Jack woke up, he immediately realized he was without his chompers but was too afraid to admit he didn't know their whereabouts. How can a guy misplace his teeth?

Appearing at the breakfast table with a modest grin, he quietly gummed his coffee, often getting up to wander around aimlessly.

"What'cha looking for, honey?" Mary inquired.

"Just wandering," he replied.

"You look like you're missing something."

"Nope."

"Maybe we can help," she offered as Jack wandered out the back door and into the alley. Mary sat smugly at the kitchen table along with Lee and Larry for nearly a half-hour before Jack ventured back into the house, his head hung in shame.

"Did you find what you were looking for at Benjie's?" she asked without even breaking a smile. She had played out the torture game to her advantage.

"No," he said in a hopeless tone.

She handed him a wrapped handkerchief. "The next time you're too toasted to keep track of your teeth, you can fish them out of the lake."

By that summer, the Great Lakes Surf Club had all but disbanded due to lack of interest. Everybody was getting older, getting their driver's licenses, and getting more interested in the opposite sex. Outside of the core group of passionate surfers, most of the guys found more interest in cars, hunting, and team sports. With male memberships dwindling, the girls, who were the cornerstone of the group's appeal, drifted to cheerleading, dance, and theater. All that remained of the original Great Lakes Surf Club were its founding members, Lee and Larry, along with a handful of dedicated friends including Jeff Schultz, Rich Kuitert, and Kevin Groh. Deciding the monthly rent on the garage wasn't worth the hassle, the group went nomadic, often congregating inside the Williams family garage on weekends. Without the inherent structure of being part of a club, the boys looked to each other to fill the down time between ideal surfing conditions. Kevin was looked upon to entertain the group at any cost—even if it meant jeopardizing his personal safety.

For a bunch of kids without any money, trying to kill each other for fun seemed like legitimate entertainment. If Kevin injured himself but didn't die—like when he rode the cardboard boxes down the hill at a breakneck speed—it was a cool stunt. Since he hadn't killed himself in the line of entertainment yet, nobody gave much thought as to what to do in the event that he maimed or annihilated himself. Everybody just kept pushing the limits of human mortality.

As the boys got older, games of touch football in the backyard were no longer exhilarating enough on their own. An amalgamation of tackle football and rugby had intensified into a "kill the guy with the ball" mob mentality with everybody jumping on whoever wasn't fast enough to run away. When trapped underneath the bottom of one of those mounds of humanity, Kevin actually broke his shoulder but didn't die. For the next eight weeks while Kevin's arm was in a sling, the playground ran amuck with "kill the guy with the ball."

While waiting for surfing conditions to improve, the boys discovered a towering willow tree that hung over the Sheboygan beach. The tree was ideal for climbing, and since it featured a branch nearly twelve feet long with another branch forking off from it (known as the "killer branch"), it was perfect for swinging. At first, the boys took turns launching themselves off the killer branch, often accompanied by their best Tarzan yell.

As they grew more daring, two of them would sit on the mature branch while the third grabbed the end of the weaker willow branch. The two boys not hanging on would aggressively swing the branch back and forth as hard as they could, turning it into a bucking bronco with the rider swinging nearly twenty feet in either direction. Letting go at the wrong time could result in a gruesome death since the rider would be thrown nearly fifteen yards into jagged rocks, prickly shrubbery, or ice-covered, frozen sand.

So when Kevin was holding on and shrieking, "Stop, stop, I can't hang on!" Lee and Larry just kept swinging him to and fro. When Kevin launched off the branch thirty feet in the air and crashed awkwardly into the killer branch that ricocheted him into a five-rotation somersault before settling into a sand dune, the Williams twins thought they had sliced him in half. Rushing to where his body lay motionless, the foursome of Lee, Larry, Rich, and Jeff looked hoping for any indications of life.

Just as the boys were about to begin preparing funeral arrangements, a weak groan emanated from Kevin. "That really hurt, guys."

All four boys began celebrating. "That was awesome!"

Even Kevin, convulsed in pain, couldn't help but smile. "Yeah, that was pretty awesome."

"Okay, who's next?" Larry joked as he assisted Kevin to his feet.

While helping their ailing compatriot walk home that afternoon, the boys felt immortal. Despite all the crazy, dangerous things they'd done in their short lives, they always survived. Luck, they felt sure, was always on their side.

Which might explain their decision to sneak into the C. Reiss Coal Company, a local manufacturer that shipped coal, wood,

salt, and building materials along Sheboygan's southern shoreline. For a bunch of bored teenage boys, the facility represented
a "forbidden playground." On Sundays, the facility was closed
and empty, its employees enjoying their weekly day off. Lee and
Larry, along with Kevin, Jeff, and Rich, peered longingly over the
front gate. In those days before surveillance cameras and private
security patrols, the compound was accessible to anybody willing
to jump the fence onto the property.

Discovering that the company's loading dock was outfitted
with a conveyor belt that led to the second floor, Lee determined
that by hitting the "up" button, they could ride right into the
building. Once inside, they climbed up and down a maze of stainless steel ladders and stairways through the labyrinth of catwalks
hanging nearly five stories above the factory floor.

When the fire extinguishers were discovered, it was every
man for himself as the boys blasted each other with baking soda.
Nearly one hundred feet above the fleet of trucks, pickups, steam-
rollers, and forklifts as well as the huge contraptions used to unload them, the boys' hand-to-hand combat resulted in everyone
getting covered in white sodium bicarbonate foam.

Having run the extinguishers dry, the trespassers focused on
figuring out a way to ride the parked vehicles below. Much to
their delight, keys were left in all the ashtrays. Commanding the
wheel of a seven-foot-tall, heavy-lift forklift, Larry chased Lee
and Kevin in their much smaller four-foot-high steamroller. The
game of forklift tag soon led to races across the factory floor before venturing outside into the shipyard along the Lake Michigan
shoreline. For hours, the boys raced through a makeshift obstacle
course of coal mounds, conveyor belts, and parked trucks.

With Lee at the wheel and Kevin trailing, the two exited the
storage structure in hot pursuit of one another, heading for the
courtyard area. With only a chain-link fence separating them from
the city street that ran parallel to the company's frontage road,

both of them spotted the police car driving in the same direction and at the same slow speed on the other side of the fence. The cop looked at them in disbelief. Lee and Kevin stared dumbfounded back at him. Everything seemed to be moving in slow motion.

The immediate thought of being busted crossed Lee's mind. Kevin's too. As with most teenaged boys faced with the prospect of getting arrested, they maximized their lack of judgment by jumping off their forklifts and racing back toward the loading dock. Abandoned by their drivers, the forklifts continued rolling forward, crashing straight into the concrete retaining wall ahead.

The boys raced up to the second floor, sprawled onto the conveyor belt, and hit the "down" button. "Head to the beach," Lee yelled. With what seemed like a suspension of real time, the belt methodically lowered the boys toward the far side of the shipyard. Fearing it would be Tuesday before they reached the bottom, the boys jumped off the belt, like a fleeing school of tuna out of a boater's net, onto the concrete below. Reaching the fence that divided the coal company's private property from the publicly accessed Lake Michigan shoreline, the boys began to hear sirens in the distance.

"Can you believe we just drove a couple of forklifts through a wall?" Kevin asked in mid-stride.

"Where's a camera when you really need one?" Lee answered with a chuckle.

Still perplexed over what had just happened, the cop failed to notice, from the corner of his eye, the boys fleeing toward the fence, leaving him with nothing more than his frustrations while waiting for backup to arrive.

Lee and Larry jumped the fence, followed by Kevin and the rest of the gang. "Once your feet hit the sand, walk, don't run," Larry barked at them. "If we run, we're busted. Only the guilty run."

With heartbeats practically pounding through their shirts, the boys speed-walked along the Lake Michigan shoreline south. Once they cleared the C. Reiss Coal Company fence line, they headed toward town, hoping like heck to make it back to the comfort and safety of the Williams family garage.

They all knew the immediate area very well. Over the past few years, they often walked along the little utility road that ran next to the coal company's fence line as a route to and from one of their favorite Lake Michigan surf breaks. In fact, not so long ago they had enjoyed quite a bit of fun on this road, which was a favorite spot for teens looking for a quiet place to make out.

The five of them had spent an entire day with shovels digging a hole nearly twenty feet long, ten feet wide, and three and a half feet deep. When the sun was about to set, they covered their hole with broken branches and handfuls of grass and leaves. As the moon rose, spreading a soft glow on their trap, they sat off to the side in the overgrown foliage, eagerly waiting for their first victim. Knowing the earlier the arrival the more gullible the target, they couldn't help but snicker under their collective breath when the first car pulled up only a half-hour past dusk.

"Quiet, quiet," Kevin whispered from the lookout point. "It's a '55 Chevy Nomad."

As the headlights beamed through the dust-filled clouds, Lee turned to Larry with a big grin. "We've got a live one on the line."

Only the sound of the popping rocks and dirt spiraling off the Chevy's whitewall tires drowned out the giggling from behind the bushes.

Vroom! The car bellowed as the tires lost traction but stayed suspended in midair for the briefest of moments. Breaking through the cover of broken branches and leaves, the car plopped into the hole with a loud metal-on-metal thump.

The boys broke into laughter.

"It just sank, like a brick in water," Larry exclaimed.

"We better get out of here," Lee said, catching a glance at the irate driver and his female passenger. "They're pissed."

Deep enough to keep the car doors from opening, but high enough that the passengers couldn't escape through their windows in any sort of graceful manner, the hole was engineered to guarantee their safe escape. Since the fall didn't damage the car, the driver suffered only disappointment and bruised pride, knowing his night of whispering sweet nothings into his date's ears would now be spent waiting for a tow truck.

As they had done during those nighttime ambushes, the boys scurried away from the C. Reiss Coal Company via the dusty utility road, unsure where the cop had gone and how closely he was following them.

"If we get caught, don't forget your alias," Larry reminded everyone. To avoid any conflicting stories, the boys had rehearsed their alibis, which involved impersonating schoolmates they had chosen. They could recite personal information about the schoolmate—from addresses, birth dates, and phone numbers to parents' names and Zodiac birth signs—in the event the police caught up to them for questioning. If they had been half as interested in applying their talents toward high school theater productions, Sheboygan would've been overflowing with Hollywood-caliber actors.

While fleeing north along the beach, Larry, who was a couple strides ahead of Kevin and Lee, made a hard left turn inland exactly four jetties past North Point. Maintaining their brisk pace, the three boys headed up a service road running alongside a large chain-link fence heavily covered in trees, plants, and vines—foliage thick enough to obscure the "Sheboygan Zoo" service signs dotted along the fence. Overcome by a foul odor emanating from behind the fence, Kevin groaned, "What's that smell?"

Neither of the Williams brothers replied, focusing instead on their hike up the steep incline ahead. Hearing strange snorts from behind the fence, Kevin slowed to investigate. "Smells like manure," he said.

When he reached a clearing in the foliage, Kevin crept up to the fence to see what was causing the smell. On the other side, stepping out of the shadows, a smelly mass of fur nearly six feet tall and weighing over eight hundred pounds lumbered over to him. With a broken-off horn and a wicked look in eye, the meanest junkyard bison east of the Mississippi River peered at Kevin through the chain-link fence.

"Better step back," Larry warned as he and Lee stood a good ten feet away from the fence.

As if on cue, the bison thundered into a charge toward Kevin—who froze in fear and fascination. The bison bellowed as it galloped toward him at full speed before slamming its huge head into the fence, which shuddered and bent from the massive impact. Kevin raced off screaming up the utility road.

"I think he might have pooped a little bit," Larry said.

"The bison or Kevin?" Lee snickered.

"Well, we shouldn't have any trouble figuring out where he ran—just follow the trail of pee to his house," Larry said, pointing to a thin line of wetness that led up the road.

Laughing harder, Lee said, "The buffalo bit never gets old."

Larry agreed, adding, "At least until the zoo takes away his credit card so he can't charge anymore."

They sauntered up the service road alongside Kevin's freshly tinkled trail before heading into the myriad alleyways and residential streets, undetected by the understaffed police force. Since Sheboygan maintained one of the lowest crime rates in the nation—a place where people felt safe enough to not lock their doors—it wasn't surprising they only had to use their acting skills

with Kevin that day and not with the police. Once again their luck
had held out. They had enjoyed a fun day wreaking havoc at an
empty factory, had been chased by the police, and had come out
of it unscathed with another great story to tell.

Somewhat shaken by their close brush with the law, Lee and
Larry decided to spend the rest of the summer hanging out in the
family garage with their buddies, swapping stories and listening
to music. While the Beatles dominated the airwaves that summer, the Williams garage rocked to the guitar-driven melodies of
Duane Eddy, Link Wray, and surf-rock pioneers Dick Dale, the
Bel-Airs, and the Pyramids. The rapid guitar picking and driving
beats seemed to pull the sound and feel of the ocean right into
Sheboygan.

    With lots of free time on their hands, the boys began refining
their amateur weatherman skills. By calculating basic information provided by local television, radio, and newspaper weather
reports, they discovered that the two principal factors meteorologists used to predict wave conditions were temperature and
atmospheric pressure. Deciphering those levels not only determined how major air masses passed across the continent, but
also indicated air molecule movement, resulting in how much
wind there would be at any given surf spot. With this method
for predicting ideal surf sessions, often accurate up to five days in
advance, the boys itched even harder to get back onto the water
with the winter surf season quickly approaching. But nobody
could predict the series of events that would leave Lee watching
his friends surfing from the shore.

    During that summer of 1969, Lee Williams lost his appendix,
not in a gambling bet, but rather during an emergency appen-
dectomy. For the freshman at Sheboygan South High School,
the initial operation was a success. But as with most emergency

surgeries, the timing couldn't have been worse. Jack and Mary had just finished packing up the car for their annual camping trip up north. Delayed for three days, Jack finally decided Lee had recovered enough and persuaded the doctors to discharge him from the hospital with the promise that "Lee will do nothing but relax during our trip."

As soon as the Williams family cruiser pulled out of the hospital parking lot, Lee proved to be as impatient as his dad. He began to build his case to do everything he planned to do while camping—surgery be damned. His constant nagging made the four-hour car ride from Sheboygan through Green Bay and across to Minocqua downright grinding on Jack, Mary, Larry, and Lee's camping buddy for the weekend, Kevin Groh. By the time Jack pulled the car into the lakefront campsite, Lee had talked his parents into letting him and Kevin go out on the boat under the condition he couldn't fish or do anything to aggravate the stitches.

As the rotting wooden boat pulled away from the dock, Lee promised, "I'm just going to sit here and enjoy the nice weather while Kevin fishes."

With not much doing out on the water, the boys relaxed in the serene setting. "I could get used to this," Kevin said.

"Too peaceful for me," Lee said. "Sitting around makes me nervous."

Then, an hour later—BANG!

"Fish!" Kevin shouted as his rod bent violently in a deep arc on the cusp of snapping. As a long, dark shape pulled hard at the bait while racing alongside the boat, Kevin swerved his fishing rod toward the portside. Summoning all the strength he could muster within his fifteen-year-old frame, he couldn't control the lunging fish as it writhed in erratic figure eights. It thrashed and splashed and then leapt into the air. Seeing the size of the fish, Lee shouted, "What is it?"

Focused on fighting the fish, Kevin just shook his head. "That's gotta be over forty inches long," Lee said.

The flailing fish surged up out of the water again, pulling against the lure in its mouth.

"It's a muskie," Kevin blurted through clenched teeth. "They're not called the freshwater shark for nothing."

After the powerful fish pounced back into the water, crashing through the glassy surface, it raced away at almost thirty miles per hour in hopes of breaking from the hook. Then it exploded out of the water again, silhouetted against the setting sun. Following a fifteen-minute battle between hand and fin, Kevin drew the muskie close to the boat, though the feisty fish was still unwilling to concede as Lee lowered the net into the water. Lashing out in a last bid to escape, the muskie showed its massive jaws and teeth to Lee, who tried to wrestle it into the net.

"How do I lift the thing up without losing my fingers?" he said.

"Chicks dig scars," Kevin offered. Lee managed to haul the netted fish into the boat without bloodshed.

"Okay, where's the camera?" Kevin asked proudly. "We gotta get a picture of this for bragging rights."

"Camera?" Lee asked.

"How else are we going to prove we caught a muskie? This is a once-in-a-lifetime achievement."

As Kevin practiced how he would stand with his trophy catch for the photo, Lee sheepishly mumbled, "We left it in the car."

"You left it in the car?" Kevin shouted.

"What are you getting all angry for? You never get hostile like this."

"I've never caught a killer forty-seven-inch muskie before."

"I'll vouch for you," Lee offered.

Kevin shook his head. "Gotta have a picture. Nobody'll believe us." Then he took a deep breath and was about to lower the fish back into the water.

"Let's show my folks," Lee said. "Everybody will believe them. I'll keep the fish underwater while you drive the boat back. We can set it free there."

"Deal," Kevin said.

By the time the boys returned to the dock, dusk had settled in and the last rays of the setting sun reached over the horizon. Jack and Mary were lounging on their plastic folding chairs, listening to the radio and reading the evening newspaper.

"Wow, that's quite a catch!" Jack said.

But when Mary saw it, she screamed.

"Mom, it's just a fish," Lee reassured her.

"You're covered in blood!" Mary cried out. She pointed to a wide bloodstain on Lee's white shorts.

Lee looked down to where his appendix used to be. "I split my stitches!"

"We've got to get you to a hospital." Mary bolted from her chair to find the car keys.

"We're in the middle of the North Woods," Lee said. "It's so far away the only thing that ever hassled Al Capone up here were the mosquitoes." He knew a trip to the hospital would bring a quick end to his vacation. "It's no big deal. The bleeding will stop in a minute."

A professional nurse's aid, Mary wasn't about to take medical advice from a teenager. She marched her boy straight into the car with a towel wrapped over the bleeding wound. At the hospital, doctors soon determined the scar couldn't be re-stitched because it had already been stitched once, leaving them to butterfly-stitch it shut. The recovery time on the new appendix scar forced Lee to avoid any physical activity and, more importantly, kept him out of the water for two months. For Lee Williams, that was purgatory.

Left to miss out on the prime surfing conditions, Lee grew increasingly frustrated and depressed. While Larry and their mutual

Larry posing with
his 10-foot, 2-inch
Wardy with double ten-
ounce volan glass and
thirteen redwood balsa
stingers in 1969

friends went surfing every weekend, he was left under his mother's strict supervision at home, and he knew better than to cross her a second time.

To escape his boredom, Lee bought a Super 8 motion picture camera with some of his paper-route money, knowing he'd be laid up for quite some time. Friends bought him film as "get well" gifts, and he soon found himself standing on the Sheboygan shoreline, looking to experiment with his new toy. In his viewfinder, Lee spotted Larry, Kevin, Chuck Walker, Rich Kuitert, and Jeff Schultz, all patiently waiting for the next great Lake Michigan wave. As the rolling film hummed through the camera, Lee enjoyed his new status as an amateur filmmaker.

For the next few weeks, Lee captured some of the earliest known motion pictures of Great Lakes surfing in existence. Though Super 8 cameras and film at that time did not feature sound (which arrived in 1973), Lee experimented with creative camera angles that caused the surfing maneuvers of Larry, Kevin, Chuck, Rich, and Jeff to leap off the celluloid frames. The grainy, washed-out footage captured the boys' pure exhilaration of surfing Lake Michigan—emotions that still photographs could never reveal. For that brief time while Lee was on the sidelines, or shorelines in this case, he unknowingly contributed to the legacy of Sheboygan's early days of surfing. But as soon as his doctor allowed him to return to the water, Lee put down his camera and grabbed his surfboard without hesitation. He was a surfer at heart, not a filmmaker.

Whenever the surfing conditions weren't optimal on the water, Chuck Walker's dad let the boys take out his sixteen-foot Starcraft boat. "If you can get it in the water and pay for the gas, have at it," he told them. That summer, the sight of a half-dozen teenage boys dragging a boat on a trailer down the streets of Sheboygan without a car was not uncommon. Pulling it along like a rickshaw, the boys would have had a hard time convincing an inquiring Sheboygan police officer that the boat wasn't stolen, if their paths ever crossed.

Once they got to the beach, they were left to drag the boat across the sand into the water—no easy feat with the twenty-five horsepower engine strapped to its back. With the smell of burning gasoline in the air, the garden of bubbles created in the water by the boat's engine signified that the Sheboygan surfers could begin towing themselves from behind on their surfboards. Holding onto a tow-cable, much like a water-skier, while accelerating to speeds of eighteen to twenty-four miles per hour, they began performing very primitive edging techniques. When they moved outside of the boat's wake, they gained speed as the rope tightened. Rapidly cutting back toward the wake and with the assisted acceleration, they caught air when they hit the boat-generated ridge of water. Long before the days of computer-generated hydrodynamic fin and integral molded rail designs, the Sheboygan surfers were unwittingly part of an underground movement across the globe that would became known as wakeboarding.

While the origins of the sport and its exact name have been hotly contested throughout its brief history, one aspect has stayed the same—ever since surfers have had access to motorboats, they've been towing each other around on surfboards. From those inauspicious early days, wakeboarding has become one of the fastest-growing board sports in the world. Akin to snowboarding and skateboarding on the water, it has since become part of the pop culture lexicon after ESPN's X-Games added it in the 1990s. Crowds couldn't get enough of the boarders' acrobatic flips and 720-degree turns, and the sport took on a terminology all its own with tantrums, backrolls, scarecrows, boardslides, half-cabs, and whirly-birds.

Thanks to their ingenuity, the Sheboygan surfers turned what would've been lackluster days on Lake Michigan's quiet waters into adrenaline-filled wakeboarding adventures. And when summer faded into fall and then into a hostile winter, the boys were caught in a war of attrition as they tried to maneuver the boat into the water over ice-covered beaches. As if signifying the end to their wakeboarding season, the peaking ice shelves along the shoreline began breaking off to form jagged, free-floating icebergs.

When ice shelves formed along Sheboygan's shoreline by November, the handful of daring souls with the skills and guts necessary to ride among the icebergs and slushy outcroppings began squeezing into their eight-millimeter wetsuits and waxing their surfboards. The same conditions that enticed Lee and Larry Williams to start surfing again were exactly why Sheboygan's five miles of coastline never received the sort of tourist-trampled traffic their surfing counterparts in Hawaii, Indonesia, or Tahiti received. With the nearest ocean over seven hundred miles away, frostbite, not shark bites, had become the Lake Michigan surfer's most dangerous enemy.

Over three hundred miles long, one hundred miles wide, and covering twenty-two thousand square miles of open water, Lake Michigan has rarely been referred to as a lake by local surfers, but rather an inland ocean. Considered to be the most-often-surfed Great Lake due to the numerous cities and beaches along both its western and eastern shores, Lake Michigan's bustling metropolises of Milwaukee, Chicago, and Gary, Indiana, are home to approximately ten million people, more than one-fifth the total population of the entire Great Lakes basin. Though it lacks the thousands of miles needed to build ocean-like waves, Lake Michigan, with 1,180 cubic miles of water, is the only lake scientists have documented to have small, lunar tidal effects. Peaks in water levels come twice a day on Lake Michigan, just as in the oceans, but the inch- to four-inch changes are often marked by far more substantial water level shifts driven by winds. The small but deeply rooted surf culture is dependent solely on wind-generated waves, often nine seconds apart, whereas the ocean's are normally twenty-one to twenty-three seconds apart.

Surfing in Sheboygan is as multi-dimensional as the lakes themselves—part extreme sport, part science, and part therapy. The Great Lakes feature over eleven thousand miles of coastline, which is more than the entire east and west coasts of the US combined. These inland oceans host the highest surfing on earth, with surfers on the western end catching waves some six hundred feet above sea level and those on the eastern end riding waves at nearly two hundred and forty feet above sea level. The freshwaters of the Great Lakes pose several differences to the saltwater-filled oceans, not least the nearly twenty percent decrease in board buoyancy that forces surfers to compensate with longer, thicker boards, up to ten feet long. With the majority of surfers equally split between

Lakes Erie and Michigan, followed by Ontario, Huron and Superior, the Great Lakes surf spirit goes beyond regional or even national boundaries.

Centrally located along nearly four hundred miles of Lake Michigan coastline, the Sheboygan shores receive waves that blow in from every direction after developing and energizing themselves across nearly two hundred miles of open water. By comparison, Chicago, which is one hundred twenty miles south, only receives decent waves from strong north winds because of its location on Lake Michigan's southern tip.

Also influencing a wave's size and shape are the constructive interferences located at the end of the water's long journey. Nearly all the best surf spots on the Great Lakes have a sandbar, a jetty, or, in Sheboygan's case, both. As the swirling turbulence of waves excavates a trough on a sandy lake bottom, Sheboygan's offshore sandbars are continually reformed and relocated as sand is carried and eventually deposited toward the beach. Jetties are manmade structures that extend perpendicular to the shore, often designed to influence currents and protect shorelines from the constant battering of waves. Sheboygan has both a north and south pier, which were constructed of reinforced concrete, steel, and boulders. Placed in strategic locations, they interfere with normal wind and wave patterns, contributing to the oncoming waves' size and shape while forcing waves to follow new paths toward shore.

Since Sheboygan's natural topography juts out five miles into Lake Michigan, winds of at least twenty to twenty-five miles per hour across the bay between North Point and North Pier create the ideal wave conditions for those in search of an ice-cold adrenaline rush. Those conditions have earned Sheboygan the reputation for getting bigger, better, and more plentiful surfing waves than anyplace else on the Great Lakes. Although the biggest waves one can sanely consider riding are around ten to twelve feet high in Sheboygan, most are in the four- to six-foot range. Anything bigger would be deemed deadly, with the really big ones, the twenty-four-footers, located about five miles offshore.

The thought of riding big waves was all Lee and Larry could talk about as Christmas vacation neared. Walking home from school one blustery afternoon, they were flagged down by their mother, who was waving her arms profusely at them nearly four blocks from home. At first they feared something had happened to one of their older brothers, or perhaps Dad had been injured at the shipyard. Their fear switched to excitement when they got close enough to hear her cry out, "It's here. You've got a package, Lee!"

Lee's new surfboard had arrived from the Soul Surfboard Shop in Huntington Beach, California. The board had artwork featuring two angels overlooking an elegantly dressed queen, exactly as pictured in the catalog he had ordered from a few months earlier. With the entire holiday break ahead of him, Lee was going to surf the daylights out of that board, regardless of the grim weather predictions.

The next afternoon, Lee, Larry, and Kevin found themselves at the edge of an icy embankment overlooking the perfect, six-foot glassy wave patterns of Lake Michigan. It was nasty cold, something like seventeen degrees late in the day, with a wind-chill factor of minus twenty-four and twelve-foot icebergs bobbing among the waves. Stepping into the water, each of them let out a yelp from the thirty-three-degree water—an uncontrollable reflex no matter how often they had done it in the past. Since the shadows were growing longer, the receding sun no longer warmed their black wetsuits, causing their bodies to chill quickly. Under these harsh conditions, the water was never inviting to beginners—only to advanced surfers and idiots. Hoping to reserve their limited energy, Lee predicted, "I give us twenty minutes before hypothermia sets in."

One by one, the three hardy souls moved deeper into the water. As they straddled their boards, patiently waiting for the next great wave, an encroaching snow squall from the west shrouded their visibility on the water to less than twenty feet. Snowflakes stuck to their moist wetsuits. Knowing their window of opportunity to surf was quickly closing, Lee bellowed, "This is cool, but what I really want is to be the first to surf off an iceberg."

"You're nuts," Larry replied.

"Good luck getting on top of one," Kevin added, knowing the ice was slicker to climb in a frozen rubber wetsuit.

Mentally projecting his path up the mass of ice, Lee approached the iceberg undaunted. At the base, he stood in chest-deep water, delicately balancing his weight on his board while grasping at the ice. His grip on it broke as waves kept washing over him, forcing him to readjust his grip several times. The waves also shifted the iceberg's center of gravity—and his own—tossing him back into the water like a bucking bronco.

"You definitely didn't inherit Dad's rodeo skills," Larry scoffed.

Unfazed, Lee asked Kevin, "Can you get me a blanket?"

Kevin raced to the shore and returned with a ratty beach blanket from his trunk. Although it got waterlogged the moment it was tossed into the water, Lee threw the blanket over the side of the iceberg. After launching his board up onto the icy shelf, Lee climbed up the blanket as if it were a stainless steel ladder. Standing atop the iceberg's peak nearly ten feet above the water, he looked down, realizing what he was about to attempt. The image of himself as a bloody pulp being peeled off the side of the iceberg overtook his initial visions of grandeur.

Lee realized he was at a crossroads that could potentially impact the rest of his life. He had to choose between climbing off the iceberg with his surfboard between his legs and live to surf another day or suicide-launching off the ten-foot-high ledge and landing in Sheboygan surf immortality.

As the next five-foot peeler rolled by, Lee grasped his board and clenched his teeth. He had only a split second to decide. Closing his eyes and taking a deep breath, he launched himself toward the wave. The frothy crest nearly bucked him off until he adjusted to find himself zipping down the face of the set's biggest wave. From where Larry and Kevin stood, Lee disappeared behind the set's first wave, but then he rolled over the top of his wave with the grace and glide of a roller coaster. Successfully riding the wave to its inevitable end along the shoreline, Lee let out a roar of triumph. He had won the bragging rights. Knowing he had flirted with death to face another day, he stood at the same icy embankment from which he announced his vision quest and cried out, "That was awesome, let's do it again!"

For the next hour, the three teenagers took turns jumping off the iceberg. Despite the snow accumulating on their wetsuits and a definite chill beginning to overtake their common sense, they continued throwing their boards up on top of the iceberg. Even as exhaustion overtook their adrenaline, they refused to quit. When the icy edges broke loose, dumping them back into the water, they lifted themselves up again, only to have another chunk of the edge break off. It was no big deal. "Just lift yourself up again," they encouraged one another, only to have another ice ball break off in their hand. The constant lifting of their waterlogged bodies onto the icebergs exhausted them, rendering their rubbery arms useless if needed to keep from drowning. But there was no time to rest if they wanted to get in a handful of runs before sunset.

So when Kevin skipped his turn to climb atop the iceberg for his last ride of the day, Lee and Larry were confused.

"What's the matter?" Larry asked.

"My board's under that ice cube," Kevin replied. "How'd you pull that stunt off?" Lee said.

"When I wiped out," Kevin said, "it got lodged underneath."

Although losing one's board after wiping out was common during the days before ankle leashes, losing a surfboard underneath a floating chunk of ice and snow wasn't. Kevin felt his brand-new seven-foot-long Hobie three-stringer pintail deserved a better fate, but he knew his options were limited.

He couldn't swim underneath to retrieve it because his old SCUBA suit would leak like a sieve, and in a few seconds he'd get the worst ice cream headache ever. As each moment passed, their core body temperatures sank slowly into dangerous territory.

"If you take two steps toward it, you'll be in over your head," Larry said. He knew from personal experience with icebergs that the chances of retrieving a board from the frozen slush were not good. No matter the size of a Lake Michigan iceberg—whether two feet, ten feet, or twenty feet high—the physics of its creation was always the same. Whenever waves crashed into it, little by little, the energy of the waves rolled back and scooped out all the sand, much like someone on a beach hand-scooping sand into piles when building a castle. With all the displaced sand forming unnatural sandbars, a surfer standing knee- to ankle-deep in front of those icebergs one moment could easily be flung underneath when a wave knocked them head-over-heels. Trapped in icy darkness only a few feet from the sandbar's edge, the surfer would be unable to decipher his whereabouts in relation to the severe drop-off, unable to touch bottom.

Those conditions would wreak havoc on the human senses. Trapped beneath the iceberg, the person's sense of direction and judgment would be immediately compromised by the frigid temperatures. Regardless of his swimming talents, he'd find it nearly impossible to navigate to the top. With the floating iceberg overhead blocking any light from the surface, the lake bottom's whereabouts would be a mystery, even if it were only an arm's length away.

With the surfer's core temperature plummeting, his body would begin shutting down in self-preservation, restricting movement of the extremities—specifically the arms and legs—to protect the heart so it can continue pumping blood to the brain. The surfer would start losing consciousness, beginning with the loss of rational thought. When the heart starts pumping blood harder and faster to keep it warmer, the body tires out faster, depleting energy levels until it is completely compromised and exhausted. Then it's only a matter of time before the person begins to drown.

Compared to the risks involved, trying to recover a two-hundred-dollar surfboard lodged beneath an iceberg verges on suicide—but never underestimate a teenage boy's belief in his own invincibility.

"I can do it," Kevin said.

Lee shook his head. "Even if you're lucky enough to swim in and find it, can you get it out of there?"

Larry agreed. "And if you can't get the board out, will you have enough time to get yourself out?"

Kevin thought for a moment, looking at the faces of his friends. Finally he said, "You're right. I'm not getting it."

Lee looked at Kevin, then at Larry, with a glint in his eye. "Well then," he said, "if I pull it out, I'm keeping it. And don't think I won't."

"Fine, I'll get it," Kevin conceded. "But if I don't come out, you'll come get me, right?"

Lee and Larry looked at each other before Larry said, "If you don't come out, there's a reason you're not coming out and we're not coming in after you."

Frustrated, Kevin shook his head for a moment before swimming over to the edge of the iceberg. Taking a deep breath, which he hoped wouldn't be his last, he dove underneath the icy monolith, leaving behind only a ring of slush. On the surface, the perception of time practically stopped for Lee and Larry. As each excruciating moment passed, the question of how long he could stay submerged in those frigid waters lessened. At what point do they go in after him in hopes of still recovering a body to resuscitate? Or do they not go after him out of risk of drowning themselves?

As the early stages of hypothermia began setting in for both Lee and Larry, their only concept of time came from how many times per second their purple lips quivered while waiting for Kevin to surface.

Both concluded he wasn't coming out but said nothing. For what seemed like an eternity, they waited in their own shivering silence, hoping for the best but fearing the worst.

Suddenly, the surfboard popped out from underneath the iceberg, arcing across the sky with the grace of a dolphin. It splashed down and skimmed onto a nearby cluster of smaller icebergs, where it came to rest alone without an owner. A few seconds passed.

"He's not coming up," Lee finally said to Larry.

Just then, the water alongside the iceberg began to stir. Air bubbles broke the surface. Kevin's eyes peeked above the waterline, peering across at Lee and Larry like an alligator. Thrusting himself onto his back, Kevin started sidestroking toward them, spitting out water in a steady, fountain-like stream of celebration.

Lee and Larry broke into uncontrollable laughter: "You're nuts. You're freakin' nuts!'

"What about 'em?" Kevin said with a grin. "They're not frozen yet."

"Let's quit while we're ahead," Larry said.

"Let's quit while we're alive!" Lee quipped.

Before heading home, the three boys ventured to Burger Chef for hot chocolate to celebrate Lee's trailblazing accomplishment

Keeping the tradition alive, Lee, left, and Kevin Groh
venture out to surf on Christmas Day, 1990.

and Kevin's near-death experience. Located three blocks from
the beach on Indiana Avenue, the restaurant was accustomed to
hosting sand-crusted crowds during the summer, but this was
the dead of winter. When the three of them lurched in like frozen
Frankensteins wearing their ice-crusted wetsuits and dripping
slush and water from their thawing appendages, the teenager behind the counter looked confused. "Can I take your order?" he
politely inquired.

Lee, Larry, and Kevin just stood there a mere four feet from the counter, close enough for the server to hear the combined chorus from their chattering teeth. "Three hot chocolates," Kevin mumbled through his frozen, purple lips.

"You boys sure look cold," the teen said.

"Cold?" Larry replied, fondling the Adam's apple on his neck. "If I was any colder, both of my testicles would've climbed up here."

Slightly warmed after watching the Burger Chef attendant turn a dozen shades of red, the three managed to saunter to the seating area, lay their surfboards against the table, and shoehorn their frozen stumps into a booth. When the server delivered the steaming hot cocoas, all three boys cupped the Styrofoam containers for a long moment, hoping the heat would run up their arms and warm their bodies. After the cocoa hit their lips, it actually burned on the way down. It could've been at room temperature, but since their core body temperatures had dipped so dangerously low, they could feel where each ounce of hot chocolate settled in their stomachs. At that moment all three agreed that it was a good day.

Chapter Five

Conquering the slush-covered waves of Lake Michigan that winter afternoon in 1970, Lee, Larry, and Kevin joined a Great Lakes surf legacy that was nearly four hundred years old. Formed nearly twelve thousand years ago after the glaciers receded north during the last great Ice Age, the Great Lakes began hosting surfers as far back as 1612 when local lore has it that French fur trader Etienne Brule surfed the waves on Lake Huron.

The modern era of Great Lakes surfing can be traced back to a local Grand Haven, Michigan, legend, when an unidentified G.I. returned home after World War II and began surfing Lake Michigan. While stationed in Hawaii, Doc "Makaha Dave" Seibold started building surfboards out of balsa wood from US Navy surplus life rafts, covering them with the crude fiberglass of the time. When he returned home to Grand Haven in September 1955, he and his longboard paddled their way into freshwater surfing history.

When the American surfing revolution of the late '50s and early '60s exploded, with movies like *Gidget* and music from the Beach Boys, dedicated individuals began experimenting with surfing on the Great Lakes from Grand Haven and Erie, Pennsylvania, to the internationally renowned group from Wyldewood. The Wyldewood Surf Club was founded in the summer of 1965 on the sandy shoreline of Lake Erie in Port Colborne, Ontario.

The American and Canadian teenagers all shared a bond known simply as "the stoke for surfing." Like many of those early experimental surfers on the Great Lakes, they also constructed their own short boards from discarded construction materials while wearing old sneakers as their wetsuit booties. Each year in the fall, the group would meet at founding member Don Harrison's house for the annual Surf Club meeting, which included screening their Super 8 surfing movies while sharing stories and photographs from the year's accomplishments. Like many of those grassroots surfing groups forming all over the Great Lakes, Wyldewood thought they were the first. In fact, surf scenes were emerging all along those inland oceans.

One of the most popular Great Lakes groups surfed along the easily accessible, well-formed waves on the south side of Grand Haven's famous pier. For kids like Lee and Larry, Grand Haven was the center of the Great Lakes surfing universe. Already bustling with a thriving subculture of bohemians living on the beach, Michigan's west coast surfing scene was where you would meet other aspiring surfers, see the newest boards, and actually walk into one of the oldest known surf shops on the Great Lakes, the Beach Point Surf Shop. When several of the local surfers began traveling to Hawaii, California, and Mexico, often bringing boards back to Michigan, they began organizing surf contests along their favorite spot known as the "Rock Pile."

While Rick Sapinski was promoting the Great Lakes Surfing Association along the shores of Grand Haven in 1966, the granddaddy of all road-trip films introduced a new generation of American teenagers to the sunny innocence and endearing spirit of surfing. Bruce Brown's documentary film *The Endless Summer* chronicled California surfers Mike Hynson and Robert August on their global quest to find the perfect wave. The film reached beyond its own surf-friendly geography as screenings in cities like Wichita, Kansas, and Syracuse, New York, found

Lee surfing near Grand Haven, Michigan, in 1990

moviegoers lined up in the snow to attend multiple showings during the dead of winter. By the time *Newsweek* named it one of the ten best films of 1966, the film had surfed its way into the collective consciousness wherever it showed. From the opening images of shimmering orange sunsets and silhouetted surfers gazing at tubing waves to the star surfers seen hiking over sand dunes under a hot African sun, Brown's film had introduced a mythology to Middle America.

The momentum of *The Endless Summer* brought forty-four Great Lakes surfers together in Grand Haven that fall to compete in the first Great Lakes Surfing Championships. But efforts to spread the word about the benefits of freshwater surfing through mimeographed newsletters failed to truly unite the various Great Lakes surfing communities dotted along the shores of Lakes Superior, Michigan, Ontario, Erie, and Huron. Left isolated from one another, they weren't united until the first published photograph of Magilla Schaus riding on Lake Erie was seen in *Surfer Magazine* in 1969—the first national recognition lake surfers received.

Although the general public dismissed surfing on the Great Lakes as an eccentric niche activity during the 1960s, the surfing revolution had spread across the entire globe—quite an achievement for a sport that began thousands of years ago when Polynesians brought the skills of wave riding to Hawaii. As the first Europeans to observe and record men riding waves on specially carved planks of wood in 1778, Captain James Cook and his crew named it "the royal sport of kings." By the turn of the twentieth century, writers such as Mark Twain and Jack London shared their wit and wisdom about the adrenaline rush generated by riding a Hawaiian wave. Soon after, Hawaii became a popular tourist destination for mainlanders, who watched with fascination the art of wave riding. Naturally, the tourists were eager to try it themselves, and many of Waikiki's native surfers became teachers, including one who became a legend among surfers— Duke Paoa Kahanamoku.

Following his gold medal win in the hundred-meter freestyle during the 1912 Olympic Games in Stockholm, Sweden, his fifth medal in four Olympics, the charismatic Hawaiian became "The Ambassador of Modern Surfing," touring Europe and the United States. Hosting exhibitions and swimming contests, Duke was known as "The Swimming Duke," "The Bronze Duke of Waikiki," and "The Human Fish." After winning the 1920 Olympic gold medal in the hundred-meter freestyle at Antwerp, Belgium, Duke and his fellow Hawaiians stopped in Detroit for several exhibitions, marking the Midwest's introduction to ocean surfing.

When a young Thomas Blake from Washburn, Wisconsin, met the legendary Duke Kahanamoku in Detroit that year, he soon became the conduit between the ancient South Pacific surf culture and America's twentieth-century watermen. Reared near the waves of the world's largest freshwater lake, Blake learned the

Lee surfing off North Side Beach's second jetty on October 31, 2009

skills of paddle-boarding and surfing as well as the art of carving boards. Developing the ability to produce watercraft in harmony with nearly one thousand years of surfing history, he was credited with revolutionizing the design of boards used for saltwater surfing worldwide.

At the time, surfboards were carved from a single plank of heavy wood, often weighing up to one hundred pounds. They were awkward and difficult to maneuver. Adopting the *aloha* frame of mind, Blake copied an ancient, largely ignored board design he saw in Honolulu's Bishop Museum. Through creative experimentation, he began producing his "hollow board" with a new wood product called plywood. Lighter and faster than the typical boards being used at the time, the "Cigar Box," as it was dubbed by skeptics, soon became famous after Duke tried and liked the design.

Besides making his surfboards, paddleboards, and lifesaving equipment easily accessible to the general public, Blake

contributed to humanity with the invention of the rescue paddleboard, which lifeguards today use on a daily basis to save tens
of thousands of lives each year. Throughout his life, Blake introduced new generations to the richness of surfing's heritage
and now is celebrated as one of the twentieth century's greatest
surfing innovators. His unique lifestyle—fusing religion, surfing,
swimming, building surfboards, healthy eating, and exercising—
became the model for the burgeoning beach culture.

By the early 1970s, the stereotypical surfer was identified as
a bronzed, blond-haired, blue-eyed wave rider whose command
of the ocean's rhythmic pulses entranced throngs of girls waiting
on the beach for even a tiny slice of his attention. In 1957, with
the success of Frederick Kohner's novel *Gidget*, which was based
on his teenage daughter's introduction to surfing, the surfing
revolution in pop culture began. It exploded when Hollywood
transformed the book into a 1959 movie and later into a popular television series starring Sally Field. As surfing's nationwide
popularity exploded stateside, there was soon no limit to how
advertisers would exploit the iconic fun-and-sun images of woody
station wagons, slick surfboard designs, and go-go dancing to the
tunes of the Safaris and the Ventures.

Media-savvy surfers capitalized on the opportunity to become
cultural icons. Filmmaker Bud Browne, who has often been credited with inventing the surfing movie genre in the mid-fifties,
surfboard manufacturer Greg Noll, *Surfer Magazine* founder John
Severson, and original surfing hotdoggers Dewey Weber and Miki
Dora became household names. As the surfing craze of the early
and mid-sixties captured the imaginations of both surfers and
non-surfers, Middle America still didn't quite know what to make
of those dedicated individuals who were surfing the Great Lakes.

Lee and Larry drew blank stares whenever they drove through
the streets of Sheboygan in a beat-up, surf-sticker-covered 1963
Ford station wagon during the summer of 1970, their Hobie, Con,

Lee and Kevin Groh overlooking Sheboygan's North Side Beach

and Dewey Weber surfboards strapped onto their Sears & Roebuck gutter-mounted roof rack. No matter where they went after a morning spent surfing, their dripping wetsuits open down to their waists, the Williams brothers attracted comments from curious onlookers, such as "Those sure are fancy dive suits" and "Are you boys scuba divers?"

Lee politely replied, "We're surfers."

Equally polite but definitely confused, the person would respond along the lines of, "How fast do you get going with the sails on those boards?"

Larry would try to explain, interjecting Gidget and Moon Doggie as pop culture references to help the person understand.

"You can't surf on Lake Michigan," the person would say.

"We just surfed the Elbow, three blocks from here," Lee might exclaim, pointing east toward the water.

If they had the time, the brothers would tell the person about surfing spots they'd heard about from other surfers all over Lake Michigan, mentioning Milwaukee's Bradford and McKinley beaches, Racine's Wind Point, known for its big antique

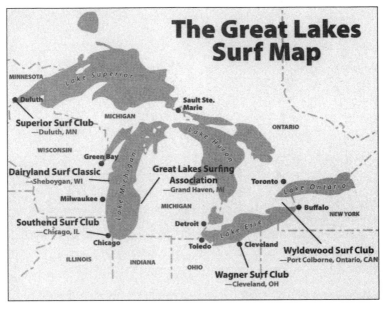

MAP CREATED BY CLERISY PRESS

lighthouse, and Chicago's Rainbow, Loyola, Oak Street, and North Avenue beaches. They'd describe the surf beach just outside of Gary, Indiana, called Whiting, known for its pounding waves set against an urban backdrop.

"It's a very surrealistic setting," Lee would say. "After paddling out, you'll see brown, stinky steel mills to your left and the Chicago skyline to your right."

Known amongst freshwater surfers as one of Lake Michigan's favorite hot spots, Whiting is near another famous surfing destination nicknamed "Shooters." Though Gary was known as one of the murder capitals of the United States, the boys weren't sure how the break earned its nickname until they heard handguns firing near them.

Larry recalled, "Here I'm ready to start swimming away from the gunfire while everybody else is standing around, drinking beer, and waxing their boards. Nobody's flinching. Not a one."

"And I'm yelling, what the hell is going on? It's gunfire, people," Lee added.

They soon found out that the building near where they were surfing was a gun club with a shooting range.

"So when you made your way back into shore," Larry explained, "the crunching noise under your feet isn't seashells or rocks, it's clay pigeons from the trap and skeet shooters."

As the listener learned about a hidden culture thriving right in his own part of the country, the boys would continue their tour, describing miles of uncharted beach breaks before venturing north past Michigan City toward New Buffalo, Michigan. Since it's only ninety miles south of the freshwater surfing Mecca of Grand Haven, New Buffalo was rapidly growing in popularity among the younger surfers. Larry and Lee described it for the uninitiated in Sheboygan: "They've got this great break on this huge marina because a bunch of millionaires from Gary and Chicago house their huge cigarette racers there and race on the open waters. So you paddle past their little marina, which is all of two

Larry surfing the Cove on his 7-foot, 2-inch Hobie long board in 1970

and a half minutes to get to the other side, and you can surf on either side, north or south. Plus, if you know there's going to be a crowd, that's where you want to be. You want to hoot and holler with your friends, push the limit, and just share—you know, the water's always 10 degrees warmer when you're surfing with friends."

To explain the lure of the sport, Larry compared it to golf. "It's not just about the drive or the putt," he'd say, "but rather the anticipation you feel when stepping up to the tee, getting that first glance of your lie when walking up to the green or lining up the putt. The nuances are in the mental preparation."

Lee related more to the adrenaline rush than the emotional quest: "As surfers, we have waves that are peaking while they're shifting. So for a downhill skier, it'd be like racing straight downhill on a mogul run and hitting those huge bumps that keep moving, forcing the skier to tuck in just the right spot if they don't want to wipe out."

Satisfied with Lee and Larry's colorful and detailed descriptions, the listener would wish them well, perhaps adding, "I'll look out for you next time I'm at the beach."

By the summer of 1970, Lee was doing quite well for himself. The sixteen-year-old was about to enter his junior year of high school and had a well-paying (by high school standards) part-time job at the local grocery store. He'd begun competing in some regional surfing events, and he took home hardware after almost every contest he entered. Larry was too preoccupied with odd jobs and a growing interest in chasing skirts to get involved in the competitive surf circuit.

When the initial novelty of beach-bunny surf movies and *Gidget*-esque fiction began to wane in popularity during the mid-sixties, the sport's appeal remained strong through competitive surfing contests, which drew audiences interested in

experiencing a sense of combat without blood during
the height of the Vietnam
War. Although surfing contests had been around since
the first time Polynesian
surfers raced each other
across a rolling wave, the
modern surfing contests
held in Hawaii and Australia and on both American
coasts were a more recent
phenomenon and attracted
the attention of magazine
writers, television produc-
ers, photographers, and
sponsors. Knowing they'd

Lee posing with his first surfboard in
July of 1970

never get rich surfing in meets, most surfers participated just to
feed their egos and fuel their images. Most serious surfers felt that
the judging of performances was as fluid—and capricious—as
the waves they rode, and so being chosen "the best" at a particular
contest didn't mean all that much to them.

Lee adapted to competitive surfing quite naturally. Beyond
being a talented surfer, which he was, he needed to be flashy—
putting lots of crowd-pleasing pizzazz into his performance to
grab the title of "champion." He learned the three skills needed
to succeed in competition: impress the judges, please the crowd,
and master the waves at the contest site. Since the surfing contest on Labor Day weekend in 1970 was held on his home waves
in Sheboygan, Lee overflowed with confidence, and it showed.
The decent-sized crowd reveled in his grace and determination as he rode the waves with panache unrivaled by any of his
competitors.

He made everything look easy. Surfing in unseasonably chilly water, he weaved through rough, choppy, and inconsistent waves. After finishing his last run, he was so numb from the cold that he could barely walk out of the water. If a competition official hadn't grabbed his board at the shoreline, Lee might have not made it to the roaring bonfire to thaw out in time for the trophy presentation.

Looking loose and relaxed in front of the enthusiastic crowd gathered at Shooting Park, Lee graciously accepted his trophy. He did his best to hide his exhaustion. While many surfers are blessed with tremendous natural ability, few had the drive Lee Williams possessed when it came to accomplishing goals.

Starting out like a million other skinny, pimple-faced gremmies, Lee developed an intense desire to become a respected surfer. He worked constantly to refine his skills. As his skills sharpened, he grew more and more confident in his ability, and he used that self-assurance to succeed in competitions.

He felt far less confident, however, when interacting with the opposite sex. He would stumble nervously through conversations with girls—if he even found the courage to speak at all. But he saw someone after the Labor Day surfing competition that inspired him to conquer those feelings. As he was drying off among a group of fellow surfers, Lee spied a spunky brunette with emerald eyes walking with her group of friends on the park's far side.

"Who is that?" he asked.

"They're from North," one of the boys replied, snapping Lee on the leg with a towel, a gesture that Lee uncharacteristically ignored.

"What's her name?"

The boy looked at the three girls walking closer to them now. "Which one?" he asked, clearly not interested.

Lee didn't break his stare at the beauty. "The dark-haired one. What's her name?"

"What do you care? Girls like her don't go for surfers like us," the boy said, rolling up his towel to give Lee another snap. "If I told you her name, you'd just embarrass yourself. Let it go."

"Introduce me. I want to meet her."

"Man, North High is a world away. Why would she want to date anyone from South?"

Lee was well aware that the north side of Sheboygan was the more sophisticated and financially entitled part of town, known for looking down upon the blue-collar south side. Nevertheless, he grabbed his trophy—in hopes it would give him confidence—and sauntered up to the spunky brunette.

"I just wanted to introduce myself as the guy who thought you were the prettiest girl in the park today," he said.

She blushed. Her friends giggled. Lee felt his confidence shaking a bit but stayed focused. "I'm Lee Williams," he said. "What's your name?"

"Michele, but my friends call me Mitch."

"Nice to meet you, Michele."

"You can call me Mitch," she said with a smile. "You were pretty good today."

"Oh, you saw that?" He waved away her compliment, feeling more confident. "Nobody cares much about my surfing."

"I think it's fascinating," she said, gazing softly at him with her big emerald eyes.

They chatted for a few minutes, the whole world dropping away as they talked. Lee had never felt this way before, and it seemed clear that his feelings were reciprocated. Hoping to continue the connection, he asked, "Do you and your friends need a ride home?"

She nodded. "A ride home would be lovely."

With the surfing events concluded, Lee left the park with Mitch and her two friends in the backseat of his 1963 Ford station wagon. As they drove along the lake toward the north side of town, Lee struggled for things to talk about.

"Tomorrow is the first day of school," he said, "so we probably won't ever see each other again. Ya know? Since we go to different high schools and all. So I just wanted to let you know how nice it was to meet you today."

He looked in his rearview mirror and saw Mitch sitting between her friends in the backseat with a tear rolling down her cheek. He stopped the car and asked if she'd get out of the car for a minute.

They stepped out. With Mitch's friends waiting in the backseat, they strolled to a nearby park. "What's wrong?" he asked.

She flipped back her hair. "I want to see you again."

Lee's heart nearly jumped out of his chest. "I would like that," he said as calmly as possible. "Can I pick you up tomorrow night to just talk about the first day of school?"

"I'd like that," Mitch said, smiling as she looked into Lee's blue eyes and leaned in to kiss him on the cheek. It was a soft kiss, warm and inviting. For Lee, it was a kiss that would change his life forever.

Larry was enjoying the Labor Day festivities with Kevin Groh and several Lake Shore Surf Club alumni. The makeshift "People's Party" reflected the times as hippies and beatniks rocked to anti-Vietnam War tunes, burning incense and selling beaded jewelry as quickly as they could weave it. The cloud of marijuana hanging over the wooded park that afternoon was probably potent enough to bake an innocent bystander in Manitowoc (about thirty miles north). Since Larry and Kevin weren't interested in participating in surf competitions, they focused on persuading friends to sneak them beers, while trying to balance their surfboards on their heads with their wetsuits pulled down to their waists. Having already drunk too many beers, Larry didn't realize his brother had left the festivities hours earlier with Mitch. He spent his night weaving through hippies squatted in the lotus position and blowing his money on beer—and later that night, blowing chunks behind the stage amps.

As the school year progressed, Lee and Mitch's relationship blossomed from physical attraction into true love. Thanks to years of surfing, Lee was a handsomely tanned, blue-eyed, sandy-blond-haired teenager. Besides his athletic build and the broad shoulders of a powerful swimmer, his ability to make her laugh made him the most romantic man Mitch had ever met. For Lee, Mitch was the perfect combination of a muse and dream girl from the moment they met. Although her petite figure, curly brown hair, and big green eyes gave the impression she was dainty and soft-spoken, Mitch immediately began holding her own around Lee *and* Larry. Playing the challenging roles of girlfriend, cheerleader, and referee when dealing with the brothers, she soon found herself in the middle of a feud between them. And they were feuding about *her.*

Larry made a habit of criticizing Lee's choice of a girlfriend behind his back. He wasn't kind in his assessment of Mitch. In retaliation, Lee dished the same criticisms when Larry began dating someone. It grew into an ugly routine—each of them bad-mouthing the other's girlfriend with "she has this issue" or "she's a that."

Since Lee was a junior and Mitch was a senior, he felt pressure to impress her at any cost, even if it meant acting against what his surfing buddies would say is "cool." He courted her with personalized sonnets, sketched drawings, and flower bouquets poached from neighborhood gardens. Since she was a northsider and he was from the south side, their relationship was frowned upon by their friends and families.

All her life, Mitch had been the good daughter, and so the qualities her parents objected to in Lee were exactly what drew

Mitch to him—he was a dark and dangerous surfer from the south side, refusing to adhere to the conventions and convictions of the conservative north side. When he introduced her to his surfing lifestyle, she was overwhelmed with excitement; it was one of the first times she had ever put her toes into Lake Michigan.

For Lee, spending time with Mitch at the lakefront couldn't have made him any happier, especially since it brought together his two favorite things in life. When the weather was hospitable, he'd bring his board along, and Mitch would sit on the shore and watch him surf. Afterward, they'd stroll along the sand and talk for hours. When Mitch couldn't join him, Lee would wrangle Larry and a couple of friends and surf whenever possible. They were becoming such skilled surfers that one former Lake Shore Surf Club member decided it was time to invite his former understudies to the Sheboygan surf party of the year.

Along with several other Great Lakes Surf Club alumni, the Williams brothers were invited to Randy Grimmer's house for his annual New Year's Eve party in 1970. Arriving at the house, which was perched at the top of a bluff overlooking Lake Michigan, they finally got to see what they'd been hearing about for years—the furnished basement decorated like a surfing museum. Surfing-themed posters, record albums, and photographs covered much of the wood-paneled walls. Surfboards, Tiki dolls, and Hawaiian memorabilia filled nearly every corner and nook. The boys felt like they'd been transported to a tropical island as far away as possible from wintry Sheboygan, Wisconsin.

Grabbing beers, they sauntered through the writhing mass of bodies dancing between the furniture to the surf music blaring on the stereo. The place was packed. With its low ceiling and lack of ventilation, it soon became a sweatbox, and beer offered the only relief from the heat. As the bodies pressed against each other, tighter and tighter, the boys continued downing beer after beer. After guzzling a tremendous amount of liquid courage, they decided to approach several of the former Lake Shore Surf Club members who were reliving their glory years amongst themselves. As Lee and Larry approached Randy Grimmer, Bill Kuitert, Rocky Groh, and Andy Sommersberger, they realized there wasn't enough alcohol in the house that night to numb their nerves. Even though everyone was a few years older, the childhood anxiety of approaching someone you idolized had yet to subside.

"You guys are really cutting it up out there," Randy greeted the boys as they approached, helping to break the initial tension.

"Thanks. The waves have been cooperating of late," Lee replied.

"Who'da thought it would be you two still surfing after all these years," Rocky said.

"You're more than invited to join us," Larry offered.

"I think our time has passed, boys," Andy declared. "We might have started the whole Sheboygan surf scene, but we're *too old* and *too cold* to keep pace with you guys."

The fact that Lee and Larry weren't being referred to as gremmies was the closest Andy had ever come to paying them a compliment. It was just the beginning of their three-hour conversation that delved into everything from their shared memories on the beach and cherished friendships long since dissolved to regrets about goals each of the Lake Shore Surf Club surfers were unable to attain.

"Enjoy the ride while you can," Bill advised. "Life on the other side of eighteen doesn't get any funner."

"The sooner you figure that out, the sooner you'll find happiness," Andy added with a toasting of his glass. As his fellow compatriots raised their glasses in unison, Lee and Larry followed.

"To your happiness, boys!" Andy proclaimed. "If it eludes you tonight in the bottom of your glass, you're still young enough to find it out there in the real world."

Larry with Lee before his senior prom

As Lee and Larry reached the bottom of their frosted beer mugs, they couldn't help but notice through Randy's picture window the Lake Michigan waves crashing down below.

After Mitch graduated from high school and left for college in September of 1971, she returned to Sheboygan on weekends to tutor Lee as his graduation approached. Since he was far from being a stellar student, she labored over his essays with elaborate corrections and comments while he tried to distract her with comical attempts at seduction. But she was serious and sensible enough to withstand them, at least in public. She had already earned a reputation as a driven young woman headed toward a brilliant academic career.

As their high school romance evolved into an adult relationship, Larry found his snarky comments about Mitch falling on deaf ears as everyone began accepting her as family. The only thing keeping them from getting engaged was Lee's continuing reluctance to commit—a hesitancy that led to several full-blown arguments during his senior year of high school.

Following a long night of drinking at the local bars, Larry jumped into the backseat of his brother's car, in need of a ride home. As the car pulled out of the lot and into traffic, Larry was surprised to hear Lee and Mitch in the front seat launch into an alcohol-induced argument. Mitch chastised Lee, saying she was tired of his sarcastic responses to her inquiries about getting married. For Mitch, Lee's lack of commitment was no laughing matter.

As the argument intensified back and forth, so did their weaving across lanes of traffic. Hoping it would all end soon, Larry shut his eyes and shoved his thumbs in his ears. If only he could manage to keep his booze-soaked brain from spinning in a million directions for the last few miles. He was so desperate to get home safely, he actually considered going to church the next morning to offer thanks if he survived the ride.

After fifteen minutes of trying to drown out the fight in the front seat, Larry noticed the car was no longer in motion. Opening his eyes, he saw that they were waiting for a train to pass. He took the opportunity to say, "I'm out of here" and bail out of the car, landing on the gravel shoulder.

Jumping to his feet and racing past the long line of cars waiting for the train to pass, Larry realized he didn't know where, exactly, he was. Doubling back toward Lee and Mitch, he passed their car and headed toward the passing train. "What the hell is he doing?" Mitch said, interrupting the fight with Lee.

As the train sped by, Larry grabbed onto one of the railcar's ladders, fleeing the scene into the darkness of night.

"What did we just see?" a stunned Lee asked Mitch.

"Your brother just hopped a train," she said with a sigh.

Knowing they were on Sheboygan's north side with the train heading south, Lee turned to Mitch. "I've got to go find my brother. We can continue this conversation tomorrow."

Disgusted, Mitch turned away from Lee, not speaking to him once during the remainder of her drive home. Following the silent trek to her house, Lee spent the drive back to his house trying to figure out where Larry could have ended up. Pulling up to the house, he saw that all the lights were off, meaning Larry had yet to make it home. Lee settled himself on his parents' front lawn to wait. If Larry were alive, he'd have to walk across the yard before crawling into bed.

Across town on the clattering train, Larry held tightly to the rusty metal ladder, but he could feel his grip loosening. Disoriented by the wicked combination of alcohol and adrenaline, he decided to jump off before he fell. Thinking he saw a familiar landmark, he leapt, slamming onto the ground and rolling into somersaults that, when he finally stopped, left him a discombobulated, dirty mess.

Instead of feeling relief that he hadn't rolled under the train wheels, he stood up to see that he still didn't know where he was in his own hometown. He looked around hoping to recognize something—a store, a street sign, a neighborhood—but it all looked strange. Then he did what most incoherent men do when unsure of their whereabouts—he started walking in a direction that seemed right.

After fifteen minutes of aimlessly wandering through the residential streets of Sheboygan, Larry saw a taxi that had just dropped off somebody in the neighborhood. He ran for it and jumped into the backseat. The taxi driver waited in silence for the drunken kid to tell him where to go. Larry said nothing, savoring the relief of having a way home.

"Where to, buddy?" the driver asked.

Larry was about to give his home address—1415 South Ninth Street—when he realized his wallet was gone. It was sitting either on the bar or in the backseat of Lee's car. But he desperately needed to get home.

"Got an address?" the driver snapped.

Larry nodded. With as much ease as he could muster, he said, "1514 South Tenth Street."

The cab shot off down the street. When it pulled up to the address Larry provided, which was one block from his parents' house, he jumped out with the promise of returning with the fare. Going around to the back of the house and cutting through the alley, Larry ran home, leaving the driver to wait, conceivably forever, for the fare.

When Larry reached the house, his bizarre journey grew even weirder. He found a trail of empty beer cans along the sidewalk leading to where Lee had pushed a reel lawn mower across the front yard just a little earlier. With several freshly cut rows behind him, Lee had been at it for a while.

"Picked a fine time to cut the grass," Larry said.

Lee looked up. Filled with both relief and annoyance at his brother, Lee just shrugged. "Every man needs vices when they're stressed. Mine are beer and lawn care."

Larry smiled. "Looks like you're mowing down the beers as fast as the grass." He felt guilty for worrying his brother with a stupid stunt like hopping a train. "Sorry for—"

Lee raised his hand to stop him. "I screwed up with Mitch. She dumped me 'cause I won't marry her."

Larry wasn't sure what to say. Though the news shouldn't have been surprising, he was shocked that Mitch had finally had enough.

"Whenever she tries to get serious," Lee continued, popping a fresh beer, "I can't help but make some asinine comment. Tonight she basically said crap or get off the pot." He managed a lopsided smile. "I guess I screwed up for good this time." He knew he wanted Mitch more than anything in the world, but making a lifelong commitment was beyond him. And he couldn't push through his own stubbornness to apologize for the mess he had made.

"Hey, everything happens for a reason," Larry philosophized. "You just gotta ride this wave out and see where you wash up. If you force things, it'll just keep dumping on you like a gnarly thunder-crusher."

For the next few hours, the two brothers sat on the grassy embankment, trying to comprehend how their lives had begun taking them in directions they no longer seemed able to control.

"All I ever wanted was to find a decent job, start a family, and grow old with someone special," Lee said, wiping a reluctant tear from his eye. "But not today! Not now! Is that too much to ask?"

"Take your own advice, and follow the path you feel most destined for," Larry replied. "Me, I want to make a difference in the world. Do something that'll immortalize me in the surfing community. Maybe like visiting all those great coasts they surfed in *The Endless Summer*."

"Don't be stupid," Lee said with a smirk. "We're stuck here, and you know it. So how, exactly, are you going to make a difference? By trying to convince people until you're blue in the face that Sheboygan is the Malibu of the Midwest?"

Larry stood up to head inside. "You're just pissed off at yourself," he said. "Why don't you quit complaining and do something about it?" He headed up the steps and into the house, closing the door behind him. Lee watched him go, feeling completely alone in the world. No one understood the conflicting emotions he felt, wanting Mitch but wanting her to wait, to let him live a little bit before settling down. Was that really so hard to understand and really so much to ask?

During the final months of his senior year, Lee tried to hide the pain of losing Mitch by flirting with cute girls who hoped to be her replacement. He also made a handful of attempts to win back Mitch, but not once did he address the core issue of their breakup. He just couldn't make himself vulnerable enough to tell her his most intimate feelings, leaving her to wonder what their relationship could have been.

His natural response to make the pain go away as quickly as possible was to spend as much time at the beach as possible. Lee could compartmentalize his feelings when focused atop his board and riding the next Lake Michigan wave. "I can deal with that mess later," he would tell himself. But as the holidays approached, the emotional weight that was burdening him began to fester into his daily demeanor.

By New Year's Eve, Larry sensed his brother was growing increasingly depressed and frustrated. So as a distraction, he and Kevin took Lee with them when an encroaching storm system was creating some ideal surfing waves on Sheboygan's north-facing beaches near the cove. Grabbing their wetsuits and boards out of the garage, Lee, Larry, and Kevin headed straight for the sand. Navigating across the bluff's frozen mudslides, the boys risked their lives before they even made it to the lake. The path was treacherous even for someone who knew his way to the water; for three over-anxious guys groping almost blindly in the encroaching dusk, it seemed a sure bet for disaster.

Somehow, they made it down to the beach.

The soft glow from the nearby streetlights cast shadows on the cresting brown waves. Though thick from the churning sand, the waves seemed surfable as they rolled toward shore. Filled with all the false confidence adrenaline can provide, the three boys cried out in solidarity as they ran toward the water, "Who needs a girlfriend when you've got these waves?"

Seconds later, all three were clobbered by a thundering wall of water—and another and another. With their feet pulled out from under them, they were jack-hammered into the lake bottom. Left to suck mouthfuls of water while being twisted by wave after wave, they had no idea if they were being shoved toward shore or spun into open waters.

After another wave slammed Lee's face into a sandbar, he realized the beach had to be near. Thrusting his hands against the lake bottom, he rose to his feet and saw the beach was only ten yards away.

Making it to shore, still filled with enough adrenaline to ignore their brush with death, the Williams brothers and Kevin retrieved their boards. As their ice-water-soaked wetsuits clung to their bodies, they paddled out past the breakers to calmer waters, nearly one hundred yards offshore. Perched on their boards while silhouetted against the rolling waters, all three could feel the unspoken tension. There was no contingency plan if things went terribly awry. On a December afternoon in Sheboygan, no one would be in earshot with them surfing so far from the shoreline.

The boys got into position as a promising set of waves approached. They anticipated who would claim the first available wave, knowing the surfer closest to the curl received the right of first refusal. The set soon washed out, leaving them to straddle their boards and admire their reflections in the rolling waves.

"Looks like we could be waiting five or ten minutes for the next set," Lee said as he looked out at the darkening horizon behind them. But not a moment later, his eyes widened at the sight of big gray waves rising in the distance. "Malibu wave!" he yelled. "Malibu wave! Party wave!"

The oncoming set of three or four oversized waves, which were bigger than the rest of the set that were often referred to as the "three sisters" by sailors, meant all three boys could cut up the waves together. For the next fifteen minutes, the rolling waves continued and they took turns riding solo or in tandem. Still gasping for air after another exciting set, Larry was the first to sit up on his board. "This is so surreal," he said while paddling back into position. "We're probably the only people surfing on any of the Great Lakes right at this very moment."

With Kevin and Lee getting ready for the next set, Larry couldn't contain his enthusiasm. "This is what life's all about," he said. "Following your passion. Living your dream!"

"Speak for yourself," Lee responded, suddenly turning serious. "I'm not living my dream. The party is over."

"What are you talking about?" Kevin asked.

"It's time we grew up," Lee snapped. He talked about owning a home, getting married, and starting a family. His abrupt change in mood caught Larry and Kevin off guard.

"Whoa, you're starting to sound way too much like an adult," Larry said.

"I can't spend the rest of my life delivering newspapers, bussing tables, or working part-time at the supermarket. It's time I start earning my keep."

Larry didn't think it was just the pressure of becoming an adult that would cause Lee to speak in such a foreign tongue. "Mom and Dad will let us live at home rent free for as long as we want," Larry said. "Who could ask for anything more at this point in our lives? We've got surfing and we've got each other."

"Sounds pretty good to me," Kevin chimed in.

"Not to me," Lee said, slapping the cold water with the flat of his hand. Floating on the lake, he suddenly realized what he wanted to do. Even in the increasing darkness of the setting sun, he could see Larry and Kevin staring at him, shivering, still startled by the change in mood, which just a few minutes before had been so full of fun. Still straddling his board, Lee sat upright and looked at his twin brother. Then he said, "I'm going to win Mitch back."

Third Wave

Chapter Six

Lee wasted no time in making good on his promise to "win Mitch back." Leaving Larry and Kevin at the beach, Lee went home to get some dry clothes and raced across town, knowing each moment wasted catching his breath was one less he'd spend with her for the rest of their lives. He tracked her to a corner bar, but when he stepped inside he saw her with another guy. He stood in the doorway, his insecurities overwhelming him. Could he have walked into a more nightmarish scenario? Lowering his head in defeat, he turned to walk outside, pausing in the doorway while muttering, "I don't care. I don't care. I really don't care!"

Then he clenched his fists and turned around again. He walked up to Mitch, took her by the hand, and looked past her eyes directly into her soul, and said, "Let's go," with the same confident determination he felt whenever riding atop Lake Michigan waves.

Without even acknowledging her date, Mitch got up and left with Lee, the two of them heading into the frigid Sheboygan night and the rest of their lives.

Over the next few months, friends and family rarely saw Lee. As soon as he graduated from high school in 1972, he began working at a locally owned family grocery store. Doing everything from stocking shelves to wrapping pork chops at the meat counter, he knew he had found a job that catered not only to his passion for surfing, but also to the love of his life. When not working, he spent the majority of his time with Mitch as their relationship continued to flourish.

Feeling snubbed, Larry avoided conversations about his brother.

When friends mentioned Lee—or when Jack and Mary brought up his name at the family dinner table (where Lee rarely was seen these days)—Larry said nothing, pretending not to hear. Distancing himself from Lee and Mitch, Larry spent his time with a handful of surfing buddies who had yet to leave for college. Avoiding questions about why his twin wasn't on the beach with them, he ignored his feelings of abandonment, saying only, "He seems to have better things to do with his time."

The summer of 1974 was filled with backyard barbecues and lakeside cookouts in the Bratwurst Capital of the World. Hardly a weekend passed, rain or shine, without the smell of charcoal smoke filling the air as every charitable, religious, and team fund-raising group in Sheboygan sponsored a brat fry, which had nothing to do with frying the meat and everything to do with grilling it. But none could compete with the pomp and circumstance surrounding the granddaddy of them all, Sheboygan's Bratwurst Days.

Lee and Larry took great pride in their hometown's most famous export, the homemade bratwurst. Usually called a brat—which rhymes with *hot*—the German sausage is made in a variety of flavors using beef, pork, or veal that is finely chopped and poured into a sausage casing along with spices. Sometimes milk or beer is added for flavoring. It was made popular in Sheboygan in the 1920s, where every butcher shop boasted its own special recipe. The brat's popularity quickly spread throughout the region. It gained national attention in the early 1950s when it was served at Milwaukee Braves' baseball games. By the end of the decade it had become a backyard favorite throughout the country.

In 1974, brats could still be found hanging in a handful of old-fashioned butcher shop windows around town. The Sheboygan Brat Days festival had outgrown its modest origins from over twenty years before, and overflow crowds could sample from nearly fifty beer and brat stands that lined the downtown district's sidewalks. But for the first time since they were teenagers, the Williams twins wouldn't be attending the festivities together. Larry decided to go with his friends after a morning surf session, and Lee wouldn't arrive until later that afternoon when Mitch finished tending to her garden.

As a local band played a polka version of "Come Fry With Me" in front of the Sheboygan post office, Larry stepped away from the tent with a beer in one hand and his first brat of the day in the other. The brat's buttery juices began dribbling out of the hard roll and down onto his shirt just as he was about to devour it. He couldn't help but chuckle, "Looks like I just got my Brat Days souvenir."

Instead of using a napkin to clean up the mess, Larry wiped his greasy face with a shirtsleeve. He took a long swig from his towering glass of amber-hued Huber beer and saw Lee and Mitch walking toward him. After they exchanged some awkward pleasantries, Lee announced to the group of mutual friends, "We're getting married." Holding Mitch's hand, Lee asked Larry, "Will you be the best man?"

Without a pause, Larry said, "No. You're too young to get married."

Silence fell over the group as everyone felt embarrassed. Larry took a drink of beer and added, "And I won't be standing up in your wedding either."

"Why not?" Lee asked.

"Because I don't like the bitch you're marrying."

Mitch burst out crying and hurried away into the sea of people at the festival.

Taking a deep breath, Lee extended his hand as if he were a politician still hoping to solicit a vote on the campaign trail. "I appreciate your honesty," he said.

The brothers shook hands. Around them, their friends stood in stunned silence, waiting for the brothers to bust out laughing, admitting it was all a joke.

"That's it," Larry sneered. "Do I need to explain myself further?"

Larry's behavior didn't go over well with his friends, who all said, in their own way, "That ain't cool, Larry."

Refusing to admit he was out of line, Larry walked away, leaving Lee behind with their friends as the polka band started up "Roll Out the Barrel."

For the next year, Larry and Mitch tried to be civil when forced to be together at family functions, but they always managed to find a reason to argue over the most mundane topics. So it was no surprise that on April 12, 1975, Lee and Mitch were married with Larry sitting amongst the guests rather than standing in the wedding party. Moving into a modest two-story house on the east side of town, the newlyweds were just three blocks from the beach. The life Lee Williams had dreamt about while courting Mitch during high school had become a reality. He was about to grow old with the woman of his dreams and couldn't have been happier.

Larry had quite a different perspective on life after high school. Following his 1973 graduation, he spent little time focusing on the future and most of it living in the present. As a nineteen-year-old living at home rent-free, Larry had a lot of independence from his parents, who only required him to abide by two simple rules: "Go to work every day—no excuses. And when we get up in the morning, your car better be in the driveway, regardless of how late you were out the night before."

His weekdays were spent behind the wheel of eighty-ton locomotives at the Kohler Company, transporting across the factory
compound loads of vitreous china clay, which would be manufactured into various plumbing implements and toilets. He found
himself with his pockets full of "adult money" and lots of free time
to spend it, which he did, usually at bars and social clubs in the
area. As one of Sheboygan's more notoriously eligible bachelors,
he measured relationships in weeks and months instead of years,
riding the social cyclone of being a serial dater.

Larry didn't fall head-over-heels in love until he met his fem-
inine equivalent, a fellow serial dater with a temper and sarcastic
wit to match his own. They met at a bar on Sheboygan's Michigan Avenue. After he offended her with one of his typical booze-
induced comments, she slapped him as hard as she could across
the face. He was impressed with her fiery attitude. She was impressed that after she hit him he didn't let one ounce from the two
beers he was holding hit the ground. From that moment forward,
Larry and Barbara were attracted to one another.

Their relationship caught fire and grew quickly. They got engaged on her birthday, November 6, 1976. Less than a year later,
on his birthday, November 5, 1977, they got married. "It'll be neat
having a wife whose birthday is the day after mine," Larry joked
at the wedding. "After celebrating my birthday, we can celebrate
our hangover on hers."

Larry made surfing less and less of a priority in his life. Barbara wanted to move inland, which meant Larry would be living
away from the water for the first time, and he found surfing to
be more of a hassle. He blamed the inconvenience of driving
across town for his declining attendance at the beach. Following
the birth of their son, Tanner, in 1980, Larry took a break from
surfing altogether, concentrating his free time on being a father
and husband at home when he wasn't working ten hours a day
at Kohler. Refocusing his passion toward earning a black belt,

he found himself at martial arts class two or three times a day, seven days a week.

Larry drifted away from his friends at the beach. The sight of his longboard hanging from his garage rafters, covered in a thick layer of dust, would always spark a snarky remark from Lee, who would tell him, "Surfing is like the mob, bro. Once you're in, you can't get out."

Brushing off the comment, Larry would claim he was focused on more important things in life. It's been said that every surfer becomes a habitual wave watcher, and Larry realized the truth of that statement. Surfing was part of his identity. When dressed in Kohler Company-issued coveralls and steering one of the cranes or eighty-ton diesel locomotives, he found himself peering out the cab window toward the water. When heading home after a martial arts class, Larry would drive along Lake Shore Drive, inhaling the fresh mist. After an argument with Barb, he found his emotions cooled down quickest when he went to the beach, which had become his place of solitude, a haven for his most intimate thoughts and feelings.

While Larry tried to find peace among the waves, his brother was busy cutting them up. Lee had become a self-possessed competitive surfer in his early twenties. He surfed to win, placing in every surfing competition he entered. At first glance, his small physique, twenty-eight-inch waist, and exposed ribs didn't evoke the image of a champion surfer, especially since he was competing against bigger kids with better gear. But as soon as he began riding a wave, his graceful, laid-back, classic style won over the judges every time. After earning his first-place trophy on the infamous day he first met Mitch, he began to enter more contests, saying, "I just want to make sure last year wasn't a fluke." In two years, he collected twelve trophies. After that success, he walked away on his own terms, believing he had nothing left to prove.

Lee's next challenge was parenthood. He and Mitch welcomed their son, Trevor, into the world on March 18, 1979. Lee enjoyed being a father. When he wasn't working at the grocery store, he spent most of his time at home—helping with diapers and midnight feedings, and often spending Friday nights alone with the baby so Mitch could complete her bachelor's degree.

Trevor with Mitch after she received her master's degree

He also became obsessed with his yard. He bathed the lawn with fertilizer and water the moment the spring thaw melted away the snow. He pampered it with an elaborate sprinkler system that ran twice daily. With the enthusiasm of a child, he edged and mowed on a weekly basis— twice a week during the height of summer. If his neighbors Ben and Rosie Goltry didn't mow their lawn often enough, Lee would say, "You can borrow my lawnmower any time, Ben."

Either from living next to a lawn-mowing overachiever or from a growing sense of competition, the neighbors began cutting their lawn more often. Ben and Lee were constantly trimming maverick blades of grass that became too long or were growing outside their respective boundaries. Summer after summer, the dueling masters of the mower kept pace with one another, creating a contest nobody could seem to win but could very easily lose.

For the next decade, their wives often sat together on one of the front porches with beers in hand, gawking at their husbands' outfits. Ben often dressed in plaid Bermuda shorts and a t-shirt, covered in grass and oil stains. Lee sported a tank top and skintight white shorts, exposing his scrawny legs. When bending over,

Lee provided quite the eye-candy for the ladies, revealing his pasty white underside. "Hey, Lee!" Mitch would heckle. "Those manly Daisy Dukes of yours sure can make an honest girl blush!"

It's not surprising that he was working on the lawn when Larry stopped by one day in the middle of summer in need of some brotherly advice.

"Where's Mitch?" Larry said.

"Inside with Trevor, baking Fourth of July cookies," Lee replied.

"What's up with you?"

Larry shrugged.

"And since when do you care where Mitch is?"

"Just need to talk," Larry said.

Unsure what his brother needed to talk about, Lee said, "Okay."

"I don't think I'll ever make Barbara happy," Larry blurted out. "She still envisions us in some sort of perfect relationship model that is impossible to attain. I'm trying to give her the benefit of the doubt, but she's always blaming me because she can't have it all."

"Doesn't sound good," Lee said.

"Then she just up and leaves us a couple of times a year for two or even six weeks at a time. She eventually comes back home, but that just isn't right."

Lee gave a low whistle. They stood in front of the house for another minute in silence. He was about to offer his brother a beer when Larry started up again. "I mean, marriages have problems—whose doesn't? But I never filed them under *divorce*. I always thought we were just working through the mountains and valleys and that we'd eventually recover."

Lee nodded, not quite sure what to do. He had rarely seen his brother so emotional.

Larry struggled to share his next thought, holding back a sob. "I don't think she's coming back this time. I could see it in her eyes."

"Being home alone won't do you any good," Lee said. "You have two options. One, you and Tanner can hang out here at my house and watch the room temperature dip below freezing while you and Mitch try to carry on a civil conversation, or. . . . "—he pulled a folded piece of paper from the back pocket of his grass-stained shorts—"I got this flyer in the mail the other day and was wondering if you'd be interested in carpooling with me."

Larry scanned the paper, which announced the 1987 Great Lakes Surfing Championships in Grand Haven, Michigan. "I don't know," he said, hesitating. "I've been out of the water for four years and don't have any real intentions of going back. I'm in a different place now."

"C'mon," Lee coaxed. "I was there last year and it was a lot of fun. I think you could use some 'me' time! Tanner can stay here with Mitch and Trevor."

Larry snickered and broke into a smile. "Only if you promise to buy all my beer."

As soon as Lee and Larry pulled into the Grand Haven beach public parking lot, they had an unobstructed view of the area's renowned surf breaks and sandy beaches. Catching their immediate attention was one of the largest collections of surfboards they had ever seen, lined up in the sand like a surfer's homage to Easter Island.

"Now this is epic," Larry exclaimed. "This view alone was worth the six hours of driving."

For the next five minutes, the brothers stood alongside their car, taking in the sights, sounds, and smells of Lake Michigan's eastern shore until one of the locals noticed their out-of-state license plates.

"You wouldn't happen to be from Sheboygan?" the guy asked.

"Actually, we are," Larry said.

"How's the surfing over there? Is it for real?"

Another eager teenager jumped on top of his friend's question. "Tell us about how big the waves get over there. I bet they're some real heavies."

The conversation kicked off the weekend in which the brothers served as ambassadors for the Sheboygan surfing scene. When walking along Grand Haven's renowned Rock Pile to watch some local surfers launching off the pier with boards in hand, they came upon an older gentleman dressed in a wetsuit, a longboard under his arm. The boys recognized his slicked-back, salt-and-pepper hair and thick, dripping-wet beard immediately.

"Are the waves working for you today?" Larry asked.

"Yeah, they're curling," the guy replied, looking toward the horizon. "Where you boys from?"

"Sheboygan," they said in unison.

The guy extended his hand. "I'm Bob Beaton, but my friends call me Doc."

Lee and Larry were very aware of Doc Beaton—a living legend among freshwater surfers. He was a lifelong surfer who caught his first Lake Michigan wave as a teenager back when his father was one of the original surfers on the Great Lakes. But his reputation as a wave rider was preceded by his decade-long dedication as an advocate for pier safety, which stemmed from his role in one of Grand Haven's most horrific tragedies.

It occurred during the early evening hours of Monday, November 10, 1975, when sixteen-year-old Dan Brown was washed off the south side of the pier by a breaking wave. His friend, Duane Middleton, jumped in after him, but a vicious riptide pulled both of them farther out into the lake. Because of poor visibility, Duane lost sight of Dan, leaving Duane to try to swim back to the pier alone, where his older brother Douglas was waiting.

Doug lay down flat on the pier and reached out toward Duane, but a wave knocked him into the churning waters below, leaving all three boys wave-tossed by the forces of a heavy north wind, gusting at times up to forty miles per hour.

After surfing the big ten-foot waves most of the day, Doc, along with his younger brother, Will, and their friends Bearle Eastling and Steve White, were carrying their surfboards down the Grand Haven pier when they saw the three boys flailing in the nearby waters. Knowing that the life expectancy of a person washed off a pier into six- to eight-foot waves was less than seven minutes, the surfers acted swiftly. Bearle dove into the water first, using his board to swim out to the Middleton brothers. Doc and Steve were right behind him as the raging fourteen-foot waves and treacherous rip currents wreaked havoc on their rescue efforts. Able to reach the two boys in less than a minute, the surfers kept them afloat by linking their surfboards. Together they paddled toward shore, fighting the current with each stroke.

As the sun dipped below the Grand Haven skyline, the temperature plummeted, bringing with it the early stages of hypothermia. The three rescuers kept trying to swim back to the pier with their victims in tow, only to be pulled away by another set of thundering waves. Will shouted encouragement from shore as Doc, Bearle, and Steve strained to bring the two boys within twenty yards of the pier. Each time they got close, an aggressive rip current along the pier's south side sucked them back out into open waters, forcing them to circle back again and again.

When rescue officials arrived on the scene, they tried attaching a line to Will, who attempted to reach the five boys still bobbing above the giant lake waves every few minutes. But when the undertow started dragging him beneath the waves, Will was forced to turn back, leaving the five boys to wrestle their way through the waves on their own. Even a forty-foot Coast Guard vessel couldn't overcome the mountainous waves in the channel and it was forced to abandon its mission. As the rescue boat's silhouette grew faint in the distance, the surfers realized their victims were on the verge of giving up. Frustrated and desperate, Doc, Bearle, and Steve decided to make a break for it.

Swimming in as far as the undertow would let them, the three surfers swam hard for the beach, angling away from the pier. As they got close to the beach, heavy waves kept breaking their linked surfboards and victims apart. After a wave hijacked Steve's board, snapping his leash loose, he was without a flotation device, leaving him to flounder in the choppy surf along with his victim. When Bearle and Doc got the younger Middleton brother to shore, Bearle raced out toward Steve. Struggling to stay afloat, Steve tried to hold onto on Duane Middletown with the constant onslaught of waves thrashing over them. But by the time Bearle reached Steve, Duane had disappeared into the churning cauldron of Lake Michigan.

By the time Bearle and Steve met up with Doc and Doug Middleton on shore around seven o'clock, they had spent over ninety minutes treading for their lives in fifty-degree Lake Michigan water. As the sky darkened, police fired off flares to light up the lake's surface, but the bodies of Duane Middleton and Dan Brown were not recovered that evening.

Because of that night's horrors, Doc Beaton began a crusade for pier safety along the Great Lakes. Lee and Larry knew about the tragedy and about Doc's efforts in increasing pier safety.

"You received a Gold Life-Saving Medal from the Coast Guard for that, didn't you?" Lee asked.

Doc nodded. "I'm prouder of what I've accomplished since," he said. His work in improving water safety had saved countless lives. Through his collaborations with local, state, and federal officials, including a series of movies he produced with the cooperation of the US Army Corps of Engineers, he was able to educate the public about the overwhelming power of the Great Lakes—a power that on November 10, 1975, not only washed two boys off the Grand Haven pier, but also, at that exact hour, sank the giant ore carrier *Edmund Fitzgerald* in Lake Superior.

While walking along the Grand Haven lakefront with Doc, Lee and Larry met Oscar "Moondoggie" Wolfbrandt, who was a member of the Eastern Surfing Association's Great Lakes District. Always looking for creative ways to get more people involved in freshwater surfing, he was responsible for organizing the Grand Haven Surfing Championships that year. In an effort to increase ESA memberships, Oscar ran contests all over Lake Michigan and Lake Huron, often spreading news of the events through his colorful newsletters, long before the days of the World Wide Web.

Oscar was quite familiar with the surfing exploits of Lee and Larry Williams after years of attending ESA competitions as the district director. At a surf contest in Sheboygan, he and his fellow judges authorized thirty-minute heats, allowing surfers to take as many waves as they wanted and scoring the top three. It was a substantial deviation from the standard United States Surfing Federation's rules, which stated a surfer got only ten waves during a twenty-minute heat, with the best three added together for the final score.

That afternoon in Grand Haven, Lee rode over twenty waves in his half-hour heat—an unheard-of accomplishment in competitive surfing circles. Paddling hard for each wave, he'd catch one, get himself atop the board, and do as many maneuvers as he could fit in. As soon as the wave started to lose power, he'd kick out over the top of the wave, paddle back out, and spin the board around to catch the next wave. By the time the heat ended, he was exhausted, dragging his surfboard across the sand like a coffin filled with cement.

Oscar Wolfbrandt laughed in amazement. "You surf like a waterflea," he told Lee. "Somehow you keep riding your board without ever getting off."

Although Larry wasn't as active in competitive surfing as his brother, he was still well known around the Great Lakes contest circuit. His lack of interest in the shortboard revolution during the late sixties prevented him from competing against surfers with boards that were designed to be shorter, lighter, and more maneuverable. Raised on longboards, Larry lacked the interest necessary to learn how to surf atop what he often referred to as a potato chip. The very aggressive shortboard style of three-second rips and slashes never felt long enough for him. He preferred to stick with the classic longboard style of long sweeping turns, nose riding, and hot-dogging by lying on his back with his hands in a prayer position for a coffin ride or crouched in a deep squat with his head between his knees with both arms outstretched in a Quasimodo. Refusing to conform his style to a shortboard, Larry continued surfing longboards, much to the chagrin of his fellow Sheboygan surfers. When folks started calling him "Longboard Larry," the alliterative name stuck.

So it was only fitting that Oscar approached Lee "The Water-flea" and "Longboard Larry" Williams to host their own surfing event on the Great Lakes. Initially, Lee was apprehensive about taking on such a time-consuming endeavor. He had retired from competitive surfing knowing the commitment that went into organizing and coordinating an event of that magnitude. Always the optimist, Larry was intrigued. Hosting a surfing event in Sheboygan would provide him an opportunity to reconnect with his old passion, not only as a participant but as an ambassador for the sport he loved. Larry couldn't contain the possibilities racing through his fertile imagination.

"This is our opportunity to make a difference and give something back to the surfing community," Larry told his brother.

After a short discussion, they agreed to hold a Sheboygan surfing event the next year on Labor Day weekend. "It's the end of the summer and the beginning of a Midwesterner's freshwater surf season," Larry said in explaining the odd choice of dates to Oscar. "It's the perfect weekend to host the biggest surf party on the Great Lakes."

Back in Sheboygan, the boys' wives offered a lukewarm reaction to the news about the Labor Day surfing extravaganza. Barbara used Larry's re-emerging interest in surfing to spend more time with her barhopping friends. She refused to help him in any way with the event. Mitch was a little more supportive of Lee but feared that organizing an event of such magnitude with his brother would create further stress in all of their lives.

After putting together the plan for the event, Lee and Larry faced the enormous task of broadcasting news of it across the Great Lakes through word of mouth and surfing-organization newsletters. Word spread slowly, and they received minimal feedback. To jumpstart publicity, the brothers invited many of their surfing friends and colleagues to a midwinter party, where they talked about the upcoming event. From the beginning, the Sheboygan Labor Day surf party was to be a gathering of surfers from all five of the Great Lakes, a place to share stories and photos and celebrate their passion for freshwater surfing, a passion only surfers could truly understand.

When asked if Wisconsin's unpredictable weather could turn the Labor Day weekend into a bust, Lee began to get anxious. What if there are no waves? What if people who don't know how to surf showed up?

"Are you kidding?" Larry reassured his brother. "Who doesn't love spending a day at the beach?"

Even for the most casual surfer, the "Surfers Only" party would be an inexpensive investment other than the cost of a basic board, leash, and wetsuit, all of which would be nearly five hundred dollars—and which many of them already had. The waves, of course, would be free. Feeling less confident about the event's

success than he acted,
Larry went to bed that Friday night before the event's
first day in 1988 hoping
someone other than him
and his brother would be
attending the inaugural
Dairyland Surf Classic the
next morning.

As dawn broke across   An early Dairyland Surf Classic logo
the glassy waters of Lake
Michigan, a ray of sunlight peered directly into Larry's bedroom,
awakening him. Despite suffering from a splitting headache, he
rolled out of bed and ventured downstairs. With the smell of bar
smoke and stale beer still in his hair, he headed to the front door
to get the morning edition of the *Sheboygan Press*. Opening the
door, he saw two Volkswagen vans, a rusty red pickup truck, and a
wood-paneled station wagon, all transporting surfboards, parked
in front of his house. He didn't recognize any of the people sitting
inside the vehicles.

"Hey, is this the home of the Dairyland Surf Classic?" somebody asked.

"I guess," Larry replied, trying to shake loose the cobwebs in
his head. "Cool," the driver of the pickup truck said. "Can I use
your bathroom? I just drove in from Detroit."

Still unsure what to think about the contingent of strangers at
his door, Larry said, "Up the stairs and to your left."

Then the phone rang, reverberating inside Larry's head like
a bag of dropped marbles. He answered the call with his typical
greeting of "Aloha." The voice on the other end wanted directions.

"To get to Sheboygan from Interstate 43, just take Highway 23
east until you get wet," he told the caller. "We'll be there in about
an hour. You can't miss us."

In that groggy moment, the first Dairyland Surf Classic began. No pomp. No circumstance. Just a handful of guys waiting outside Larry's doorstep at six o'clock on a Saturday morning looking to catch Lake Michigan's first surfable Labor Day weekend wave. For the next three days, Lee and Larry, along with twenty of their newest surfing buddies, toured the Sheboygan breaks in search of waves that, unfortunately, never seemed to materialize. Little did they realize that it was the first of many wave-challenged Labor Day weekends—an annual tradition that was rivaled only by the Surf Classic itself. The lack of waves did little to discourage the newly assembled group of surfers as they bonded, sharing their various perspectives of what surfing on the Great Lakes meant to them.

At night, the surfers lined up their boards along Larry's garage and grilled hamburgers and brats. As the beer flowed from the keg stashed in the corner of the backyard, the surfing stories grew more boastful and adventurous. With all the surfers staying at Larry's house, the beds and couch were quickly claimed, leaving most of the guests curled up on the floor alongside the fireplace. Some brought tents and pitched them on the front lawn.

Mornings were spent recovering with a healthy cocktail of coffee, eggs, orange juice, more brats, and a handful of aspirin. The hardcore types washed it all down with beer. Lee's daily "Dawn Patrol" included four cups of coffee and four eggs neatly wrapped around four hot dogs. Whenever a guest asked why he covered his breakfast in salt, Lee replied with annoyance, "Would you disrupt the washing machine if your clothes were getting cleaned every morning?"

Following another day of minimal waves on Lake Michigan, the Dairyland Surf Classic on Sunday night became an unofficial film festival as everyone gathered around the living room television to watch all the hippest surf movies. Classics such as *Morning of the Earth*, *Storm Riders*, and *Blazing Boards* never seemed to grow tiresome as the Great Lakes surfers relished the outlandish surfing exploits immortalized by many of their Hawaiian and Californian wave-riding icons such as Miki Dora, Greg Noll, David Nuuhiwa, George Greenough, and Daniel "Mr. Boogie" Kaimi.

While those films served as colorful conversation starters, the first highlight of the evening came from Oscar-nominated Bruce Brown, who had combined his two passions—surfing and filmmaking—into visual and narrative storytelling with his epic *The Endless Summer*. The film was originally screened on the beach city surf circuit in 1964, two years before it became a general release. As mentioned earlier, *The Endless Summer* chronicled Californian surfers Robert August and Mike Hynson as they traveled the world for three months in search of the perfect wave. Its theme—if someone had enough time and money, he could follow summer around the world, thus making it endless—reached both its core surfing audience and mainstream America. Playing against the traditionally stiff and formal documentaries of the era, *The Endless Summer* became widely recognized as both a cultural and commercial success, setting the bar that all surfing movies in the future would try to reach.

Another mandatory film at that first Dairyland Surf Classic was the coming-of-age movie *Big Wednesday*. Set within the romantic surf lifestyle in Malibu during the 1960s, the film was both a critical and box office disappointment. Pulled from theaters after grossing an underwhelming $4.5 million, the film starred William Katt, Gary Busey, and Jan-Michael Vincent as party-loving surf heroes who are forced to face the adult realities of friendship, love, marriage, war, and death between the summer of 1962 and the Great Swell of 1974. It wasn't until the movie was released on home video that it became a cult favorite, reaching its niche audience of surfers—including Lee and Larry Williams—who related to the three main characters despite living over two thousand miles away from the movie's Southern California setting.

To add authenticity to the movie, world champion surfers Jay Riddle, Peter Townend, Ian Cairns, Billy Hamilton, Bruce Raymond, and Jackie Dunn appeared as stunt performers to execute the black diamond runs. Captured by legendary surfing cinematographers, including Bud Browne, the surfing sequences had an exciting pace that had never been featured in a mainstream surfing movie before. The action scenes left Larry Williams' living room abuzz with excitement.

When Gerry Lopez, who was considered the world's best tube rider, made his cameo appearance in the film, the room fell silent. Although he was chosen by director John Milius to bring closure to the aging characters' surfing life, Lopez had already been responsible for single-handedly ushering in the shortboard revolution after winning the prestigious Pipeline Masters competition in 1972 and 1973. Spending the better part of the next two decades designing boards that allowed surfers to survive the vertical drops and thick tubes of Pipeline, Lopez also became one of the first surfers to sponsor team riders with free boards, in part because they didn't have the money to buy them. His legacy was not lost on any of those in attendance at the Dairyland Surf Classic that first year.

"He can sponsor me anytime," Kevin Groh said. "I've always been a charity case on the waves."

"Bro, could you even fathom what you'd say if you actually met him?" Larry asked.

"I can't imagine what it would be like to be recognized, wherever you were in the world, by surfers wanting to shake your hand," Lee said.

Appearing in the finale of *Big Wednesday*, Lopez rides with an elegance and style all his own. In the film, he represents the next generation of surfers who are taking the place of Katt, Busey, and Vincent's characters as they prepare to go their separate ways. While watching Lopez's relentless conquering of another wall of water, Vincent's character comments, "Lopez. He's as good as they always said he was."

Busey's character solemnly responds, "So were we."

All the aging surfers in the room could relate to that sentiment. It was the perfect conclusion to the first Dairyland Surf Classic, and everyone in the room demanded that Lee and Larry promise to hold it again next year.

What began as an excuse to reunite a bunch of buddies to surf, swap stories, watch movies, and drink beer doubled in size the next year. As word spread outside of the Great Lakes surfing community, folks from California, Canada, and even Hawaii arrived in hopes of testing the big waves on the big lake. Recognizing the public's growing interest in freshwater surfing, over the next few years Larry began doing interviews for local radio and newspaper reporters, promoting Sheboygan as "The Malibu of the Midwest." He tried to dispel the stereotypes about hardcore surfers defending their turf against outsiders and newbies.

"In Sheboygan we'd sooner lend you our board and teach you how to surf," he'd say, "since the odds are pretty good that within two minutes of meeting one of us, we'd be friends. And you'd be even more popular if you brought beer."

Local media outlets, which originally covered the Dairyland Surf Classic as a curiosity, started to realize the attitude surrounding Sheboygan surfing was changing. As soon as the Sheboygan and Wisconsin boards of tourism started promoting the event with billboards, paid advertisements, and feature articles, the Sheboygan surf scene began earning respect.

The new popularity, however, seemed to taint the Dairyland Surf Classic's innocence. Instead of Lee and Larry knowing everyone who came, they noticed dozens of surfers who didn't smile or wave at them. More and more tourists visited, leaving their candy bar wrappers and empty cigarette packs behind as proof of their attendance. To see the surfers in action, groups of inlanders walked out onto Sheboygan's mile-long pier. While wipeouts were still the big subject of post-surfing conversation, there was a deeper fear that the event's exclusiveness was dying in the eyes of some of the wave riders.

The traditionalists grew frustrated. What had started out as a celebration of why they loved surfing in the first place—the opportunity to be individuals and avoid the status quo—was turning out to be the "in" thing to do. No longer interested in participating in the spectacle that the Dairyland Surf Classic had become, some traditionalists refused to attend. Although sympathetic to these concerns, Lee and Larry vowed to continue organizing Surf Classics as the ultimate showcase of freshwater surfing. They had created something special and, in their own way, had begun to make a difference, just as they had always dreamed they would do when they were starting out. Future generations of Great Lakes surfers would enjoy what they had created. They also focused on teaching two members of those future generations—their sons Tanner and Trevor.

Chapter Seven

With Larry's passion for surfing reinvigorated, he introducing his son, Tanner, to the sport. An energetic ten-year-old, Tanner had already developed a keen appreciation for skateboarding and BMX dirt bike racing. His highly skilled hand-eye coordination helped him make a smooth transition into skimboarding, body-boarding, and surfing. Father and son became inseparable with every available moment spent at the beach or in the garage designing their toys. Larry turned every activity with Tanner into an education. If dad were going to spend eighteen hundred hard-earned dollars on a single-speed bicycle and drop an additional thousand dollars on a rolling toolbox, the two of them were going to construct it piece by piece from the ground up.

"Listen here, kid," Larry would tell Tanner. "If you want a bike this expensive, you're going to learn to work on it."

Those mechanical skills helped elevate Tanner into a local hero among the younger kids in the neighborhood as he fixed their skateboards, bikes, and surfboards. He knew all the lingo from reading every surfing, biking, BMXing, and skateboarding magazine in circulation. Just like his father a generation earlier, Tanner dressed to be different, often wearing tassel hats in the middle of summer, pulled down as low as possible. His long hair hung down to the middle of his back. He copied West Coast fashions as portrayed in his magazines, having Larry drive him down

Larry and Tanner surfing Lake Michigan in 1988

to Chicago for the big baggy pants, shoes, and stylized flannels. Tanner was not only dressing the part of a rebellious surfer but also separating himself from the wannabes who tried to emulate the scene just because it was popular.

From the first time he caught his balance on a longboard, Tanner strived to become a professional surfer. Willing to get out on the water under even the most harrowing conditions, he showed no fear when passing on smaller waves for the opportunity to surf the bigger, more challenging ones. He developed what is often called the "athlete's mental edge." Dedicated to practicing the five Cs—curiosity, consciousness, confidence, calmness and consistency—Tanner began to exceed even his own expectations.

After months of coaxing, he was finally able to convince Larry to enter him into his first surfing competition in the late summer of 1990. Tanner had just turned 10. At Grand Haven, Tanner competed against the best surfers throughout the Great Lakes, regardless of age. "The Gales of November Contest," as it was nicknamed, would play no favorites that weekend as an aggressive near-shore wind swell created treacherous water conditions, which even the most skilled Lake Michigan surfer considered "monster scary." The wind gusts blew so hard only one surfer had made it past the outside break before Tanner's first run.

When he dropped his six-foot *ripstick* shortboard into the water, he was determined to paddle past the break. Navigating through the choppy surf without capsizing should've earned him a trophy for perseverance alone, but the only hardware Tanner was focused on taking home was for being the best competitive surfer on top of the waves that afternoon.

On his first run, he made it past the break, much to the judges' surprise.

Patiently waiting for the next big wave to roll toward him, he trusted his instincts as several sets passed him and petered out before reaching shore. When his wave approached, he maneuvered for the take-off, chased it down, and felt the tail of his board lift, thrusting him forward into the first drop. Cutting through the wave, he followed the rolling sections as they evolved and dissolved. His near-perfect ride ended with a kick out and fast turnaround to paddle back into the choppy surf for his next wave.

On his next run, Tanner wiped out almost immediately after his surfboard got caught in a thirty-five-mile-per-hour wind gust, punching him in the mouth. The wicked smack echoed all the way to shore, where Larry cringed alongside the rest of the anxious parents in attendance. When Tanner washed up on shore, he was still dazed from the hit. With blood gushing from his nose, he sat on the wet sand wearing the blank stare of a prizefighter struggling to survive the late rounds.

"Aren't you going to do something?" one of the attendees asked Larry. "He's still in the competition," Larry replied. "I'm not going to touch him and jeopardize his eligibility. It's all part of the breaks."

Ignoring his parental instincts to comfort his son, Larry remained in the designated viewing area. Tanner just stared out at the water, not even blinking as the wind and waves flopped and churned his orphaned board alongside him. As he glanced over at it, the board flipped up, slapped him in the mouth, and knocked out his two front teeth.

Larry couldn't contain himself, and he raced to his son with a cold towel, which he placed over Tanner's bleeding mouth. "We're going home," Larry said. "Get in the car."

"I thought we were camping tonight," Tanner mumbled through his bloodied, broken teeth. "You promised."

"We've got to get you to a dentist."

"We're five and a half hours from home," Tanner argued.

"This isn't a democracy. You don't get a vote. Get in the car!"

On the ride back to Sheboygan, they stopped only for gas. When Larry finally connected with the dentist from a filthy gas station pay phone during the middle of the night, he was able to arrange an appointment for nine o'clock the next morning, a Sunday.

They had Tanner in the dentist's chair and fitted for caps before the first Mass of the morning let out. In typical Williams fashion, less than an hour later, Tanner and Larry were riding waves just as large as the ones in Grand Haven. Since freshwater waves of that magnitude were rare, how could Larry keep his son from pursuing his passion after surviving such a traumatic situation?

Just as devoted to fatherhood as his brother, Lee introduced his own son, Trevor, to the beach, taking him for strolls along the Sheboygan shore as soon as he could walk. A weekend never passed without father and son wandering along the shoreline to skip rocks, examine driftwood, or collect washed-up bottle caps.

On the drives to and from the beach, Lee would point out where the surf was breaking or how the weather was going to affect the waves later in the day.

While driving north along Third Street one afternoon, Lee pulled the car to the shoulder to gaze from the bluffs with Trevor. As the seven-year-old eagerly jumped out of the car, he slammed his hand in the door. When the automatic lock clicked shut, terror overtook the boy. He couldn't move his hand; he couldn't cry; he couldn't even scream. When Lee noticed that his son wasn't at his side enjoying the view, he looked back at the car and saw Trevor peering at him through the window with a look of terror.

Lee vaulted over the hood of the Impala with the grace of an Olympic gymnast, stuck the landing, and quickly unlocked the door. By that point, Trevor was a slobbering and screaming mess. As his hand swelled up like a cupcake, Lee gunned the gas. Making every light along the way, they were able to apply ice to the throbbing appendage before the swelling got too severe. Fortunately, Trevor's hand didn't suffer any lasting damage. He recovered so quickly, in fact, that a few weeks later Lee got Trevor on top of his first surfboard.

From an early age, the Williams brothers would dress their sons in wetsuits and place them on the Lake Michigan shore break alongside each other with bodyboards in hand. Although the boys were less than a year apart in age, they couldn't have been more different. Tanner was long and lean with the build of an athlete. Trevor was muscular and shorter. Tanner filtered everything through the adrenaline rush he felt each time he straddled a wave, while Trevor never seemed to quite connect on that physical level. Rather, he possessed a more sensual perspective, enjoying the sights, sounds, tastes, and smells more than the ride. Not inclined to endure extreme amounts of pain like his cousin, who was constantly getting thrashed on his BMX bike or skateboard, Trevor followed his passion for music and comedy. At any opportunity, he'd whip out his acoustic guitar and throw a handful of change and dollar bills into the empty case to encourage passersby to contribute. He thrived on the attention and laughter he received when cracking jokes between songs. In contrast, Tanner never craved the spotlight, despite being one of the most decorated surfers of any age on all of the Great Lakes.

A couple weeks after returning from the Grand Haven competition, Larry decided to head home early from work one afternoon to grab a nap before waxing boards later that night with Tanner. A short time later he awoke to see Barb standing over him with an angry look on her face.

"This isn't going to work anymore," she said. "I just left my attorney's office. You'll be getting divorce papers served in ten days."

"You're just going to leave us?" Larry said. "After fourteen years? I can't believe you're quitting on us."

"I'm out of here," she said and walked out the door.

As Larry wiped the sleep from his eyes, he followed her outside and saw that she was almost finished loading the car with her belongings.

"You really think you can do better than us?" Larry said.

She continued to load the car as if he wasn't there.

"And don't think I haven't heard how *popular* you are with the boys around town," he said.

She slammed the trunk shut, jumped into the front seat, and turned the ignition key. As the engine revved, Larry walked up alongside her window. "Tanner and I are going to make a difference," he told her. "We're going to go on living life without you, and you're going to miss it all."

By the time he finished speaking, she had pulled away, leaving him to watch her turn signal blinking back at him. She sped around the corner and disappeared.

In hindsight, Larry should have seen it coming—all the signs were there. Barb had grown increasingly distant in recent months, refusing to talk at dinner or while they watched television.

Following an ugly divorce in which he received joint custody of Tanner, Larry focused on becoming the best parent possible. Avoiding the urge to jump into some new relationship just to numb his pain, he started taking Tanner to every Great Lakes surfing competition scheduled.

Because all of the events were organized through the Eastern Surfing Association, Tanner was able to accumulate enough points that season to enter the northeast regionals in Montauk, Long Island, New York, by May of 1991. That year was the first in which Great Lakes surfers were allowed to participate in the event. A few days away from his eleventh birthday, Tanner was not only the first Great Lakes surfer to compete in that major surfing contest but also the first to finish as high as sixth in the standings. His placement earned him an invitation to the largest amateur surfing competition in the world, which was to be held in Cape Hatteras, North Carolina, in September of that year and hosted by the ESA.

Back in Sheboygan, word quickly spread that if Tanner finished as one of the top four competitors in the event, he would be able to travel around the world and surf in competitions with all expenses paid. As soon as his school recognized his accomplishments during the morning announcements, everybody wanted to talk with him. He was mobbed and congratulated in the hallways between classes. Several local television and radio stations interviewed him, and the newspaper featured his story on the front page. Through it all, Tanner seemed unfazed, dismissing it as more of a nuisance than a pleasure.

"Aren't you excited about what's going on?" Larry asked his son.

"What?" Tanner responded in a subdued tone.

"It's got to be exciting—being as young as you are with all of your accomplishments."

"Why?"

"Why?" Larry said, taken aback. "If I was accomplishing what you're accomplishing at your age, I would have been passing out from the excitement. How can you not be stoked?"

"It's cool," Tanner replied, without much emotion. He refused to allow his accomplishments to inflate his ego, as it had with some of his friends. Instead, he spent his entire summer vacation perfecting his techniques of leaning in, arching back, and standing tall atop Lake Michigan's wind-driven waves.

By the third week of September, Tanner was as prepared as he could be for the competition in Cape Hatteras along North Carolina's Outer Banks—home to the East Coast's best surf break. When he arrived to compete in the ESA's Outer Banks Surfing Championship that weekend, he was aware of the significance of his inclusion as a freshwater surfer. Founded in 1967 by East Coast surfers looking to promote, preserve, and protect the sport of surfing, the ESA only invited surfers from the Atlantic coastline from Maine through the Gulf Coast of Florida to Alabama. Prior to Tanner's invitation, Great Lakes surfers weren't eligible to compete in their national contests. As the ESA grew in size and stature, much like the reputation of the Great Lakes surf scene, it expanded competitions to include surfers of all ages and abilities from anywhere in the United States. Today the organization hosts qualifying amateur events for the American Surfing Championships, the USA Surfing Championships, and the US National Surf Team. National winners then compete across the globe through the International Surfing Association (ISA), which is officially recognized by the International Olympic Committee.

As Tanner let the North Carolina beach sift through his toes, he gazed at the pounding waves. Much like the Great Lakes, the quality of surfing in the Tar Heel State depended primarily on the numerous sandbars that allowed rolling waves to regularly reach the shoreline. Dressed in his wetsuit in anticipation of un-seasonably chilly waters, Tanner felt his experience surfing the slush of Lake Michigan provided him a slight advantage over his competitors who surfed in the more tropical water temperatures of Virginia, Georgia, and Florida.

After the horn blew, Tanner and the handful of surfers in his heat paddled into the aggressive waves. Even when the surfers found a rideable wave, they were barely able to stay balanced, often falling off into the brutal surf. Competing against nearly a hundred surfers from ages six to fifty-five, Tanner performed tricks and stunts he never would have attempted on Lake Michigan's shorter sets. Although disappointed with placing twenty-second at the event, Tanner knew he had accomplished something even more significant than winning a trophy. He had earned the respect of his ocean- surfing counterparts while proving that Great Lakes surfers could compete on a national level.

During the twenty-hour drive back to Sheboygan, Larry and Tanner talked about the challenges of their lives without Barb. Larry struggled to afford raising his eleven-year-old son on a single income.

"We can't afford to live in our house anymore," he told Tanner. "But we'll move to where you can stay in school with your friends."

"Are you sure?"

Larry nodded. "You need good friends right now."

"That's cool," Tanner said. "Thanks, Dad."

Looking his son in the eye, Larry said, "We're going to make a difference. Regardless of how uphill the journey is."

A few months later, father and son moved into a modest two-bedroom, two-story house three blocks from Lake Mich-igan. As Larry hung his favorite Greg Noll surfboard poster in

Larry and his Hobie Phil Edwards longboard in fall
of 1992

the kitchen, he couldn't help but feel the move closer to the lake
signaled a new beginning for him and for his son.

Reconnecting with his surfer roots, Larry opened his house to
any surfer passing through town that summer. During busy weekends, his house became a surfer's Howard Johnson's. His guests
loved the surf memorabilia decorating the walls, the longboard

fins dangling from the ceiling, the ornamental coral sitting on the tables, and the shark jaws hanging over the kitchen stove. For Tanner, the constant flow of people deepened his love for the sport and the lifestyle, and it also improved his skills, as surfers shared their techniques and perspectives with the whiz kid.

Some of Larry's most frequent visitors were his friends from Northern Minnesota's Lake Superior Surf Club who, when in need of a new, freshwater surfing fix, made the ten-hour drive through the night so they could arrive in time to grab the day's first waves. They'd help each other squeeze into wetsuits and wax each other's boards as soon as their cars rolled into the parking lot—all for the chance to get into Lake Michigan as soon as possible. By the time Lee and Larry met up with them just minutes after first light, those cold-water boys had already ridden a handful of waves and were waiting to catch another set. The blustery winds creating the barreling waves at the Elbow along Sheboygan's North Pier only seemed to get bigger as the sun arced across the blue afternoon sky. Although Sheboygan was often celebrated as the ideal place to surf on the Great Lakes, the water could just as easily become treacherous, as Larry found out on the ominous evening of August 19, 1991.

What had been a glassy lake surface only minutes earlier had churned into tumbling chaos as dark clouds moved over the North Pier lighthouse around six o'clock. A cold front blustered its way across the water, carving deep ridges into the Lake Michigan waves. Sheets of spray ripped across the pier, leaving no distinction between water and sky. Knowing the power of such violently unorganized waves, Larry left his board in the car, choosing instead to sit on the rocks next to a Sheboygan municipal utility beach house and sip on a beer. As the waves crashed against the pier, he noticed two boys around eleven years old running onto the pier toward the lighthouse on the far end.

"They're about to get themselves killed," he said to himself. Racing to the pay phone alongside the utility house, he called 911. "Send somebody right away before it's too late!"

Never taking his eyes off the boys, Larry saw them run nearly one hundred yards toward the lighthouse while dodging waves that exploded into the pier, arcing nearly seven and a half stories in the air over the fifty-five-foot-tall lighthouse. Realizing that the huge plumes of water would engulf the boys before help arrived, Larry chased after them.

As he reached the foot of the pier, a wave clobbered him, knocking him onto the slippery concrete, where he fell on his hip. Before he could get up, a huge wave pulled the kids off the pier, sweeping them into the harbor's raging waters. Regaining his balance, he limped toward them. He reached the five-foot utility ladder concreted into the pier and hoped it would serve as his anchor while leading him down into the churning waters that pushed the boys into the harbor. As he climbed down the ladder, he coaxed the boy nearest him, Michael Burt, to swim toward the pier.

"Come on!" he shouted. "Paddle! Swim, swim, swim! You can do it!"

Fully clothed and tiring in the cold water, Michael couldn't make headway against the strong undercurrents. Each time he came up for air, he would be sucked back underwater, unable to touch bottom, growing more exhausted with each futile stroke.

Larry reached out his hand. "Swim harder," he yelled. "You're almost here!"

Pausing for what Larry assumed was a quick breather, Michael disappeared, sinking into the cyclone of white water. Larry leapt off the ladder, grabbed the kid's wrist, and pulled him onto the ladder. "Stay here," he demanded while knotting Michael's weak arms around the ladder rungs. Larry then focused on the second victim, Aaron Levanduski, who continued to drift farther from the concrete barrier. "Come on, kid! Swim, swim, swim!" Larry cried.

Seeing the boy's arms stretched over his head, Larry thought Aaron was going to push down, lift up his head, and take a big gulp of air before swimming toward the pier. After only taking a few uninspired strokes, the boy's arms went limp, and he was pulled under, swirling around in the strong current like a toothpick. Once more launching off the ladder, Larry swam to the struggling boy and brought him to the ladder alongside his friend.

The waves pounded against the pier's far side, arcing overhead as Larry held onto both boys with his left arm and leg clenched around them while he wove his right arm through the ladder rungs. The waves crashing around them formed a wall of water receding off the pier, and the longer they held onto the ladder, the more they felt enclosed in a watery tomb. Shaking from fear and too scared to cry, Aaron stared into Larry's eyes with a look of defeat. "I can't hold on anymore," he said.

"You don't have to hold on, I've got you," Larry said. "Help's on the way."

The boy said, "But I can't breathe anymore."

He was beginning to hyperventilate, growing limper and heavier in Larry's arms. The kid didn't have much time left, and Larry, for a moment, was unsure what to do. Wondering if someone—the Coast Guard, police, fire department, anybody—was ever going to help them, he said nothing, knowing anything he said could demoralize the boys. Convinced they wouldn't survive without him, Larry refused to consider that he might die that afternoon. His son Tanner was almost the same age as Michael and Aaron, and Larry hoped that an adult in this same situation wouldn't give up, but would do everything possible to save his son.

Weaving their limp arms around the rungs of the ladder, Larry shouted, "Hold on, and don't let go," above the barrage of crashing waves. "When I tell you to come up the ladder, climb as fast as you can!"

The boys nodded.

"I'm going to see what's headed our way. Just hang on!"

After swallowing a mouthful of water, he climbed up the ladder and glanced over the top of the pier to estimate when the next set of waves would strike. A wave smashed him in the face with a force comparable to a fire hose, folding his eyelids backward and stretching all the tendons in his arms.

From his brief peek above the pier, Larry realized the same treacherous waves that were holding him and the boys prisoner were probably hampering the rescue efforts the Coast Guard and fire department were attempting from shore. Just as Larry's vision cleared, Aaron's screams pierced through the noise of crashing waves. "I can't hold on! I can't hold on! I'm going to drown."

Believing he likely would lose Aaron during the rescue, Larry told Michael, the stronger of the two, to follow right behind him up the ladder. The water washing over the surface of the pier made everything slick and weakened Larry's grasp on the boys. It would be only a matter of time before he could no longer hold onto either of them, leaving all three to freefall into the churning waves below. When the waves subsided for a brief moment, Larry shouted, "Let's go! Follow me up the ladder. Hurry!"

Interlocking all of their arms, Larry formed a chain between him and the boys. Rushing up the ladder as fast as he could, Larry pulled both boys onto the pier just as another wall of waves crashed into them. Scrambling to their feet, the three reformed their interlocking chain of arms and ran toward land. Although they were only a hundred yards from safety, it felt like miles. With barrels of water arching over the pier, spray and mist fell from the sky, hampering their visibility as much as their ability to gain traction on the slick cement.

Larry ran alongside the open water, taking the brunt of the shattering waves. Understanding a chain was only as strong as its weakest link and resigned to the fact Aaron probably wouldn't survive, he had Michael linked between him and Aaron, who ran along the leeward side.

As the three trudged across the pier's slippery surface, the rumblings of a monster wave roared over their shoulders. When they turned to see it, the wall of water smashed into them, knocking them to their knees and pushing them toward the edge of the pier. Just as quickly they got back on their feet and headed toward shore again.

"Stand still and lean into it," Larry directed. When another huge wave engulfed the group, Aaron was almost washed off the pier, his legs dangling off the edge.

Larry reached down and pulled him up with one swift motion. "We have to be faster," he demanded. "Move with purpose *and* efficiency." With waves sideswiping him, Aaron couldn't gain his balance, causing him to shuffle and stumble across the slick concrete. But he slowly progressed toward shore, with only the interlocking chain keeping him from plunging into the harbor.

Then, through the mist of crashing waves and spray, Larry saw emergency lights from fire trucks, ambulances, and squad cars. When he saw silhouettes of rescue workers and concerned citizens standing by helplessly at the foot of the pier, he realized the conditions were still too hazardous for a rescue attempt from shore. Summoning up their last remnants of strength, the trio hustled across the pier's last fifty yards.

Realizing they were out of immediate danger, though still twenty yards short of the parking lot full of spectators awaiting their arrival, Larry and the boys paused to catch their breath.

"We're going to make it," Larry told them.

The boys gushed, "Thank you, thank you, thank you. You saved our lives."

Larry said, "I don't take thanks. I only take hugs."

Michael and Aaron embraced their rescuer in a group hug. They squeezed each other tightly as their tears of relief mixed with the spraying mist from the waves that continued to crash around them. Still dizzy from the shock of the experience, Larry and the boys collected their emotions and headed toward the crowd awaiting them. As he watched the two eleven-year-olds disappear into the crowd, a police officer walked over to him and draped a blanket over his shoulders. "Are you all right?" the officer asked.

Suddenly overcome with the power of the experience, Larry said, "No," while beginning to sob. "No, I'm not."

The officer led Larry to the same rocks where less than an hour earlier he had first discovered the boys running on the pier. "What's the matter?" the officer asked.

Larry could only reply, "I almost died out there."

"Do you need anything—medical assistance?"

With adrenaline subsiding, Larry now felt pain lashing through his bruised hip. He started to tell the officer when Tanner, who was navigating his way through the crowd, called out for him. As Tanner reached the rocks at the base of the pier, he wrapped his arms around Larry in a bear hug. "Dad, I can't believe you just did that!"

Larry turned to the officer, cracked a smile, and said, "I'll be okay."

After his story appeared in nearly every newspaper as well as television and radio broadcast throughout Wisconsin in the weeks that followed, Larry became recognized in Sheboygan as the hero who saved those two boys. Restaurants gave him free meals, the bakery didn't accept his money, and even the local *Sheboygan Press* newspaper disregarded a late subscription payment, giving him the paper gratis for a couple of months.

Larry appreciated the attention but more importantly, he felt he survived the ordeal in order to serve a greater purpose. Since his friend Doc Beaton had lived through a similar experience, Larry began contributing to Doc's Great Lakes pier watch safety program by educating people about the dangers surrounding the 108 piers located throughout the five Great Lakes and collaborating on a pier watch safety video for the US Army Corps of Engineers. For his efforts, Larry received the second-highest life-saving award in the United States—the Silver Lifesaving Award from the United States Coast Guard.

When the Secretary of Transportation honored him during a ceremony at the Kohler Company, Larry joined a very small fraternity. As one of the oldest medals in the United States military, the honor can be bestowed to a member of the US military or to a US civilian who rescues or tries to rescue anyone from drowning or other peril of water at the risk to one's own life. Since it was established by an Act of Congress on June 20, 1874, the Lifesaving Medal has only been awarded to approximately seven hundred individuals—whereas the Medal of Honor, established approximately ten years earlier, has been awarded to nearly 3,500 recipients. Holding the heavy silver medal, Larry couldn't keep the tear welling up in his eye from rolling down his cheek. It eventually found its way down his chin and neck toward his proudest memento from the occasion—a shark-tooth necklace Tanner gave him only moments before the ceremony.

"Nobody's tougher than you," Tanner told him. "Not even a shark!"

As the year-end holidays approached, Larry saw a lot more of his brother, who was itching to undertake a new challenge.

"I'm going to surf the reef," he told Larry, referring to the limestone outcropping that sat in the middle of Sheboygan Bay. "Some guys from Illinois are talking about surfing it first, and that just wouldn't be right."

Lee surfing Sheboygan in 1992

The natural reef, part of the Niagara Escarpment, was quite the geographical temptation for local surfers. Because it forked out of thirty feet of water to create its own six- to eight-foot pool of shallow water, waves passing over it tripled in size under the right conditions, peeling off beautiful barrels that would last a city block. But because it was located nearly three-quarters of a mile off the shoreline, nobody had risked surfing those open waters, knowing that if something went wrong, they'd never make it back.

On Sunday, December 1, 1991, Lee stood on the frozen Sheboygan beach in very inhospitable weather conditions with surfboard in hand. "No flatlander is going to lay claim to surfing that reef first unless I freeze to death getting out there," he proclaimed to his friend Pat Brickner, who brought a camera in hopes of capturing the historic moment.

The surf was up that afternoon as Lee paddled out toward the eight-foot-tall Nunn Buoy that notified boaters of the shallow reef below. The brisk wind cutting across his face in the open waters turned his runny nose into an icicle. The exposed hair peeking out from his wetsuit hood had become sharp, frozen daggers. He knew the window of opportunity to surf the reef was limited since the time it took to paddle out was enough to bring on hypothermia.

Awaiting the right wave, he chose a glassy six-foot barrel that lasted nearly one hundred yards. Orphaning the wave before it dissolved into the Sheboygan Bay, he immediately turned back around and paddled toward the buoy. After riding out a couple of shorter waves, he returned to shore to catch a quick breather before venturing back out again.

"Did you get that?" he asked Pat, who seemed preoccupied with licking the accumulating frost off his telephoto camera lens.

Pat nodded. "It looked great," he said. "Do you want me to get a few more?"

"Just let me warm up a minute," Lee said while rubbing his hands together in a futile attempt to dry them in the frozen, whistling winds.

As the two men stood on the iced-over Sheboygan beachfront that frigid December afternoon, the faint thumping of helicopter rotors began echoing in the distance. Lee smiled. "You didn't have to arrange an aerial photo shoot," he said with a chuckle.

Pat just stared back at him.

"I didn't think so," Lee shrugged.

Since the helicopter was heading straight toward them, they grew concerned. "That's the Coast Guard!" Pat said. "They don't fly around here unless they're looking for someone."

Specializing in short-range recoveries, the orange-painted H-65 Dolphin Eurocopter swooped down toward the reef Lee had just surfed. "I think they're looking for you," Pat said. "Someone must have seen you heading out to the reef and thought you were committing suicide or something."

When the helicopter circled back for another pass, Lee decided it was time to leave. As stealthily as a grown man in a black wetsuit carrying an eight-foot surfboard on the frozen Sheboygan beach in December could, Lee loaded up the car. Without putting his foot on the gas, Pat rolled it out of the parking lot, as if revving a car engine would've been heard over the helicopter rotors. Like guilty school children absconding with the answers to an upcoming test, they made their getaway, watching the helicopter circling above the reef through the car's rearview and side mirrors.

Lee and Pat didn't discuss the events at the reef that day with anyone—not even Larry or their wives—fearing their attempt to earn some local bragging rights would turn into a legal nightmare, possibly even landing them in jail.

The incident was forgotten until three weeks later, when Lee was bagging groceries for a customer who happened to be a Coast Guard cook. "Did you hear about that guy over Thanksgiving weekend riding around the lake on a surfboard?" the officer asked the checkout girl. Lee said nothing as he bagged the groceries. The checkout girl said she hadn't heard about it. "The Coast Guard spent over ten grand bringing a helicopter up from Chicago. And they never even found the guy."

"Oh," was the only response the checkout girl could muster as Lee loaded the last packed bag of groceries into the cart. When the cook walked out the door, the checkout girl could no longer contain her grin. She looked at Lee and asked, "Do you know anyone crazy enough to do that?"

"Not at all," he said. "Not at all."

Word soon spread around Sheboygan's surfing circle that somebody had actually surfed the reef. Although everyone knew it was Lee, he wasn't about to bring any attention to it. "I appreciate the congratulations," he'd reply, "but this has to stay among us. No bragging rights are worth ten thousand bucks. The Coast Guard might want their money back."

For Lee, keeping quiet about such an accomplishment was torture. Fearing arrest for daring such an act wasn't all that pleasant either. As he always did when he was upset about something, he focused on his lawn, looking forward to the spring thaw. Pushing a mower, clipping hedges, and trimming branches brought instant gratification whenever things weren't going well. He had spent so much time on his lawn the past few years that his neighbors could no longer compete in the friendly rivalry of dueling lawns, conceding his victory.

Following another festive Fourth of July, Mitch's favorite holiday, Lee spent an entire weekend packing up her red, white, and blue party favors, themed streamers, and firecracker lawn ornaments. He knew the task of organizing the next Labor Day weekend surf party with Larry would soon be his next task to tackle.

By 1992, the Dairyland Surf Classic had evolved into a full-blown event, just five short years since its inception. No longer just a dozen friends looking for an excuse to drink beer and watch surf movies, the event had taken on a life of its own. Lee and Larry struggled to keep control of it. The increased attendance meant organizing more events, ordering more food, and working with the city of Sheboygan to reserve and permit the space accommodations on the beach since the Dairyland Surf Classic was large enough to be considered an "organized event" by civic leaders. While a lot of people saw the playful side of Lee and Larry during the Labor Day weekends, nobody quite understood how much stress was involved as they spent nearly every July and August weekend in Larry's basement planning and preparing.

The stress led to arguments between them, sometimes to the point where they were ready to start throwing punches. Then they would calm down, and the moment would be just as quickly forgotten. They moved on as only brothers can.

As this Labor Day weekend approached, Lee found himself manicuring his lawn on a daily basis, sometimes tending to it after breakfast as well as right before going to bed. His grass-stained hands were a sure indication he was feeling pressure over the weekend's growing popularity.

"Why do we keep encouraging more people to attend every year if all it does is cause us to fight?" Lee asked Larry. "Why should we put ourselves through this year after year? Why can't we keep it exclusive? You know, a surfers-only party like we originally intended."

"It's not about us," Larry replied. "It's about the love of the lifestyle. And we're responsible for bringing new people into it."

Lee nodded in silence.

"When all those kids race into the water to catch their first wave of the day," Larry continued, "that's why we do it."

Lee smiled. "Even the people who irritate the crap out of us can't ruin that."

"It can be a pain, sure, but you have to admit it's cool getting all the surfers back together every year."

Lee agreed. They had the same conversation every year— expressing their frustration but concluding that all the time and trouble was worthwhile.

A few weeks later, with the Dairyland Surf Classic in full swing, a San Diego couple arrived at the beach, fully equipped with surfboards and wetsuits rented from the local surf shop. "We've never surfed freshwater before," they told Lee and Larry, "and when we heard about Sheboygan, we planned our whole summer vacation around this weekend."

The couple was so stoked to surf Lake Michigan, they had forgotten to check the weather conditions ahead of time. The waves that year were small. But the couple showed no sign of disappointment as Larry spent the afternoon with them, tearing it up on the little two-footers. "Surfing in Sheboygan really exists," they hooted and hollered. "We can't wait to tell our friends!"

Those sorts of stories prompted visitors from around the globe to arrive in Sheboygan with boards under their arms. Lee and

Larry began promoting their hometown's attributes to national newspapers, radio stations, and television news reporters looking for the next "feel-good" story. Never once bragging about the waves, they focused on what made riding waves in Sheboygan so special—the opportunity to share their experiences and great surfing conditions with anybody willing to visit and have a good time.

"Hey, it's water. And since nobody owns it, we just share it," Larry often explained, echoing the Hawaiian philosophy of surfing. "The aloha spirit is probably at its thickest here on the Great Lakes. There is no attitude here. We share everything on the beach, from beer and food to wetsuits and surfboards."

Larry took great pride in the fact that his son was carrying on those same attributes. It seemed the older Tanner got, the more he looked up to his father despite their occasional battles over homework. Never one to be labeled a "dedicated student" by his teachers, he always struggled through assignments, knowing that if his grades weren't good enough he would be forbidden from entering surfing competitions. So when Tanner was assigned a report on his favorite hero, Larry offered some suggestions— skateboarder Tony Hawk, BMX freestyle rider Scott Freeman, or pipeline master Kelly Slater. He knew Tanner worshipped those guys.

Tanner looked up from his notebook and said, "I'm going to do it on you."

Larry was stunned. And speechless.

Tanner said, "You may not know everything, but you sure aren't afraid of anything."

Larry smiled at his son, knowing all the while that he was terrified about raising Tanner as a single parent. For the next couple of years, he combated those fears by actively participating in his development as a student, surfer, and rebelling teenager.

Larry understood how his boy was turning into a typical fourteen-year-old, consumed with all the hormones and attitude. By the summer of 1994, Tanner was already six feet tall and weighed one hundred and forty pounds. Like most teenage boys, he pushed his father away in an attempt to establish his own independence. Larry tried his best to understand Tanner's feelings while somehow keeping him on the right track.

On a warm July afternoon that summer, Larry was busy waxing a surfboard on his front porch. From a distance, he could hear Tanner holding court on the trunk of a friend's car along the curb in front of their house as a handful of his closest friends joked around. Larry always enjoyed watching Tanner with his buddies. He listened as they talked about teenage stuff—girls, music, clothes, school.

Then one of the boys jumped into the driver's seat, thinking it would be funny to race around the neighborhood with Tanner still sitting on the trunk. As the car accelerated to forty miles an hour, the driver spun a U-turn, throwing Tanner from the car and into the street.

He died right in front of Larry from a fractured skull.

Chapter Eight

As paramedics tried unsuccessfully to revive Tanner, a part of Larry Williams died on the pavement that afternoon. Watching his son being loaded into the back of the ambulance, he was consumed by anguish. He couldn't breathe. He felt nauseated but could not vomit. His baby wasn't supposed to die. He never said good-bye. All Larry could do was break down in tears as the ambulance pulled away.

A few days later, Tanner's funeral was held along the Sheboygan shoreline. Nearly seventy-five family members and Great Lakes surfers paddled out past the Elbow, Tanner's favorite break, to hold a surfers' version of a wake. The group arranged themselves in a circle and placed leis and flowers in the middle. When Lee swam forward to give a little speech, he made sure he and Larry were holding Tanner's favorite surfboard. Lee's comments about Tanner, and about the loss of a young man who held so much promise, left the group sniffling and sobbing as they spread the ashes across Lake Michigan's calm, glassy waters.

After the funeral, surfers from around the globe asked Larry if they could spread Tanner's remaining ashes across some of world's most famous surfing destinations. With Lee and Trevor's help, Larry spooned ashes into Ziploc sandwich bags and addressed them to his friends Mark Fragale in Waimea Bay, Hawaii;

Tanner's funeral on Lake Michigan

Lester Priday in Australia; and Peter Pan in Cape Hatteras, North Carolina. Additional packages were sent to those in the Florida Keys, Huntington Beach, California, and Cloudbreak, Fiji, who knew Tanner personally.

Afterward, Larry was forced to confront the paradox of grief—wanting to be free of the overwhelming pain of the loss while grasping for any reminder of the loved one. As the weeks passed, Larry's heartache spiraled into a deep depression. He struggled to eat and sleep, and often awoke in cold sweats from night terrors, feeling as if he could have or should have done more to prevent the accident. At work he managed to focus well enough to do his job operating eighty-ton steam locomotives but found himself lost, for the most part, in a fog of despair. He drifted away from his family and friends and turned to alcohol to drown the pain.

Later that summer at the annual Sheboygan Brat Days Festival, a mutual friend approached Lee and Mitch while waiting in line for cheese curds. "Your brother's in bad shape," she told them. "He's sitting in the middle of a field, drunk as a skunk, and speaking in tongues."

Lee turned to Mitch and, without saying a word, headed toward his brother. He found Larry a few minutes later surrounded by a nest of empty beer cans. "I . . . have . . . no . . . reason . . . to . . . move . . . on," Larry stuttered as tears gushed from his bloodshot eyes.

Lee crouched down and calmly said, "Let's go home."

As they sat in the car, neither one spoke. Lee focused on the road while Larry wiped away tears and tried to contain his sobs. When they arrived at Larry's house, Lee walked him up the stairs and laid him down in bed, fully clothed.

"I can't make the pain stop," Larry said.

Lee knew there was nothing he could say to comfort his brother. Larry's sorrow was one he had never experienced. So he acted on instinct, leaning in to hug his brother. For nearly an hour, he held his brother tight as Larry cried himself to sleep.

Larry awoke the next morning fully clothed, still smelling of alcohol. When he lifted his head off the pillow, his heart began its daily ache, but he refused to be incarcerated by grief for another day—which was already a lot longer than Tanner would have tolerated. Larry decided this would be the day he started moving on. After taking a long, hot shower, he combed his hair, dressed in his favorite Dewey Weber t-shirt, and decided to start the first day of the rest of his life on his favorite stretch of property on the entire planet—the beach.

Stepping off his porch and onto the sidewalk, Larry took the first of several deep breaths that morning in hopes of keeping the rush of emotions from overtaking him. Casually striding down the sidewalk, he smiled and exchanged hellos with passers-by who were unaware that each step he took brought him back to life. The closer he got to the sand and surf, the more the lake rejuvenated his senses—the sky looked bluer, the air smelled fresher, and even the waves crashing on shore sounded crisper. Arriving in time for first light, he scanned the lake to the horizon, finding a momentary peace in its vastness. He took off his shoes and walked toward the water, sensing each granule of sand sifting through his toes. It had been months since he had been in touch with the beach on such an emotional level, and he admitted to himself, "I've been away too long."

As thoughts of Tanner cruised through his consciousness, Larry understood that memories of anything, especially a person or an event, were always less than the whole. The recollection of his son's death was becoming less than nothing, leaving him with fewer mental images and feelings. He could no longer remember whole thoughts, just fragments of his surf-crazed teenager getting more waves than any kid had ever gotten on the Great Lakes. Although their briefness initially scared him, Larry's flashbacks made him smile. He couldn't help but cherish them. Coming back to Lake Michigan served as the best therapy possible for Larry to work his way out of depression. He reconnected with what made him happy.

Caught up in a reverie, he found himself standing in waist-high water, still fully dressed in his t-shirt and jeans. As each wave rolled over him, the grime of grief and months of inactivity seemed to wash off his arms and legs. Without a board, he paddled out, venturing farther away from shore as each stroke seemed part of an emotional journey that reunited him with the water. Aimlessly floating along the undulating waves, Larry

Returning to surf the lake with friends provided Larry with the best
therapy possible.

couldn't imagine a better way to spend the first day of the rest
of his life.

In the days and weeks that followed, surfing provided Larry's best
therapy. He spent nearly every weekend at the beach, hooting and
hollering with the handful of his closest friends who had been
there with him from the start. The group of guys—Larry, Lee,
Kevin Groh, Mark Rakow, Mark Wente, and Teek Phippen—
seemed to spend more time telling stories over beers than actually
surfing. Often dehydrated and physically spent after spending
nearly seven hours a day doing one of the most intense aerobic
workouts known to man, the surfers felt the only thing that could
refresh them was a cold beer. Insisting cheap beer tasted the best
after surfing, Mark Rakow raised his empty brown-and-white
aluminum can in the air and proclaimed, "From this day forward,
we shall call ourselves the Blatz Surf Team."

When Lee, Larry, Kevin, Teek, and Mark Wente raised their
cans and replied, "Here's to Team Blatz," they had no idea how

their decades-long friendship, built on surfing, had solidified into the symbolic gesture of raising a can of Blatz beer. Taking the joke a step further, Mark Rakow decided later to sew an old Blatz cloth patch onto the back of his maroon-hooded sweatshirt. Lee and Larry thought it would be fun to start issuing team jackets. Taking plain Dickies work jackets, which looked like beer delivery truck jackets, and putting large Blatz patches on the back and a smaller one on the front, they embroidered "Blatz Surf Team" in large gold letters underneath the patch. To personalize the jackets, each surfer was given a nickname.

When Larry decided to issue Lee the first team jacket for his birthday, he sewed "H2O Flea" underneath the front patch. Everyone had been calling his brother "The Waterflea" for years. Larry rolled up the jacket in an emptied twelve-pack box of Blatz and gift-wrapped it. That Christmas, Lee returned the gesture in a gift-wrapped, emptied-out case of Blatz that contained a rolled-up "Longboard Larry"-embroidered jacket.

Much like the Great Lakes Surf Club of the 1960s, Team Blatz was more about being part of a group than about operating a functional organization. Without drafting a formal charter, declaring an official set of rules, electing officers, or even being sanctioned by the actual beer company in any way, Team Blatz was born. The one rule: the Team Blatz jackets could only be gifted, never purchased, leaving only seven jackets issued beyond the original group of six who toasted one another that fateful afternoon. Whenever they begin zipping up into their wetsuits, waxing their surfboards, and putting on their leashes, those surfers wearing their Team Blatz jackets can't help but get sentimental. How often do a group of guys that have been surfing for nearly four decades still find themselves acting like teenagers about to catch their first set of waves?

When they weren't on the beach surfing or drinking beers, the members of Team Blatz would often socialize at their fellow

From left to right, Team Blatz members Mark Wente, Larry Williams, and
Teek Phippen

surfer's coffee shop, The Weather Center Café, on the Sheboygan
riverfront. While many surfers rely on buoys, local television, and
the National Oceanic and Atmospheric Administration Web site
to gather weather reports, the Sheboygan surfers looked to their
friend Teek Phippen. The café combined Teek's two passions in
life—surfing and weather. While surfers often mature into amateur meteorologists, Teek found his childhood obsession with
Mother Nature to be a valuable tool when he started surfing. Because he kept up with the newest forecasting technology, Sheboygan surfers turned to him when the local weatherman predicted
a Canadian clipper currently clobbering the Pacific Northwest
would make its way toward Wisconsin in the next couple of days.

Teek could refine the forecast by focusing on its impact on
Lake Michigan's waves. If the storm system moved slowly, for
example, the lack of wind from the low pressures would develop
less pressure on the water and create fewer waves. If the front was
moving fast and pushing everything out of the way while creating

high pressure, the heavy winds it was generating would result in choppy waves. When factoring in that the water temperature was 33 degrees with a 26-degree air temperature, those potentially cold winds over the warmer water would produce the friction necessary for the formation of the ideal surfing waves.

Since The Weather Center Café had only a handful of seats, it was perfect for lounging and conversing in small groups. Larry often found himself there late at night, guzzling quad lattes to avoid a flask of whiskey or a forty-ounce can of Pabst Blue Ribbon. When not debating weather theories with Teek or getting lost in a book, he often talked to a beautiful young woman from Boston named Kerry. As the conversations between them deepened so did their emotional connection. It was no surprise that Kerry and Larry soon embarked on a lust-filled courtship that was as hot as it was fast.

Two years later, on June 19, 1999, Larry and Kerry decided to get married at Sheboygan's Shooting Park. Since it was the second wedding for each of them, they agreed less was more. To keep things simple, word of mouth served as the main form of invitation as friends and family came from all over the Great Lakes. Guests were encouraged to wear Hawaiian shirts, board shorts, and flip-flops. While the group of around one hundred people, nearly ninety of whom were surfers, stood around the park waiting for the priest and priestess to arrive from Milwaukee, the thirsty crowd popped the keg of beer a little early. When the officiants showed up, the crowd set down their beers and watched the ten-minute ceremony. As soon as Larry and Kerry exchanged vows, champagne bottles popped and the music blared. The party rocked straight through the night.

Rather than going on a honeymoon, the newlyweds focused their efforts and money on remodeling Larry's house. Coexisting under one roof proved to be difficult during the first few months of their marriage. It didn't help that the ink on her divorce papers had barely dried, or that he was adapting to someone living in his house for the first time since Tanner's death. Nearly once a month, their wedding license managed to find itself in the trash, only to be fished out when cooler heads prevailed.

Larry was quickly discovering the pitfalls of falling in love with a woman whose Irish temper and lack of patience would not tolerate his keeping the worn-out, stained carpet he had installed when he moved into the house a decade earlier. But the carpet, for Larry, was more than just a collection of nylon fibers—it was a time capsule, a conduit to his past. It had survived years of bombardment from ketchup stains, wax burns, and drunk-induced pukings during numerous Dairyland Surf Classics, so Larry ignored Kerry's first handful of requests to remove it.

"Hey, baby," Kerry said in her thick Boston accent, "There is no way I'm buying new furniture and putting it on that crusty piece of crap. So you will be rolling up that hideous thing and redoing these hardwood floors."

"You sure about that, hon? I figure it's got two or three years left," Larry said. "We just need to give it a good vacuuming."

Kerry took a deep breath, knowing there was scientific proof somewhere that counting to ten in a moment of anger saves lives. Then she said, "The carpet goes—period."

Larry knelt down and said good-bye to his carpet. Since a hazardous waste removal team wasn't available to examine it ahead of time, Kerry wasn't sure if his tears were caused by emotion or by the aroma wafting from the carpet's underside. As soon as his moment passed, Larry grasped the carpet's loosened end along the far wall and gave it a hearty tug. Initially worried the topside of the carpet would disintegrate from years of wear and tear, he discovered the foam backing—hardened by numerous foods, fluids, and fungi—had cracked open and released all the smells of years past. For Larry, each odor-filled stain had a story associated with it—from the dried beer, cigarette butts, pizza crusts, and animal fur balls to more sand than a small beach could hold.

Once the carpet was removed, the marriage flourished. They were good for each other. Larry brought perspective into Kerry's work-heavy lifestyle, providing laughs whenever she was stressed. Kerry defused the arguments brewing between Larry and Mitch at family functions. As their relationship grew, they brought each other happiness, spending many a night talking, smiling, and whispering until their eyes closed.

When he awoke on New Year's Day morning in 2000, Larry knew the Y2k scare was just that after receiving an email from the Weather Center Café announcing it would be a good day for surfing on Lake Michigan. When Lee, Teek, and the rest of his usual surfing buddies couldn't be found, Larry headed out by himself. After kissing his wife good-bye just six hours into the new year and three hours since going to bed, Larry noticed all of Sheboygan seemed eerily desolate during his drive. Parking his car near the Elbow, he grabbed his longboard from the back of his truck and ventured across the crunching, iced-over sand toward the water. Carefully navigating over the snowdrifts, respecting the slick surface, he balanced the board on his shoulder while walking toward a break in the jagged landlocked icebergs. Dropping his longboard into the ice floes that swayed above the crashing waves, he knew his window of opportunity to surf that morning would be small. With a snow squall rolling in from the north, visibility was poor. Regardless, he paddled out, losing sight of shore, and waited for his first set of waves. As snow began sticking to his wetsuit, creating the illusion he was tarred on one side of his body and feathered on the other, he sat on his board in silence until he heard a familiar voice through the whistling wind.

Larry and his ice-covered wetsuit on New Year's Day 2010

"Happy New Year," the greeting bellowed through the fog. "I got your message, but I figured you weren't crazy enough to surf in this soup alone." Mark Rakow appeared through the mist, kneeling on an eleven-foot longboard.

"I'm not crazy," Larry replied. "But I'd be certifiable if I passed up these curling barrels."

For the next couple of hours, the two jumped off six-foot icebergs into clean five-foot peelers. Since the air temperature was just twenty degrees, along with fifteen-mile-per-hour gusts, the early stages of hypothermia left neither one of them thinking too clearly. But when Mark's board chunked into a wall of foam, he confessed, "That's enough for me. I'm turning purple and already late for a family brunch."

Larry mumbled through frozen lips, "I'll follow you in on the next good wave."

Mark gave a surfer's nod before wading back to shore, soon losing sight of his friend. As the storm waves thundered in, Larry felt a rush of adrenaline. Letting a few smaller waves pass, he picked one that offered a perfect ride to end his day. When he reached the shallows, he dismounted, noticing the icy embankment near the shoreline had grown. When he was retrieving his board, a seething white wall of foam shoved him toward shore. Crashing against the jagged icebergs, Larry found himself trapped. The icy landing where he had entered the water only a few hours earlier had frozen shut. The wall of ice between him and the shore was shaped like a frozen wave ready to curl, arcing nearly fifteen feet overhead, making it impossible to climb. Walking through waist-deep water, Larry stayed optimistic he'd find a route through the blockade of sand-covered ice.

As the storm conditions intensified, the surf pummeled against the ice floes, breaking apart gigantic chunks of ice, which crashed and overturned in the churning waves. Instead of avoiding the massive icebergs, which weighed as much as ten tons, Larry determined his only chance of getting out of the water before turning into a human popsicle would be by timing a jump onto one of them and hoping he could hold on. With his ten-foot longboard under his arm, he knew the prospects of pulling off the stunt were slim, but so were the odds he'd survive in the water much longer.

With so much water washing off the towering icebergs, he had to time his jump just right. If he didn't stick the landing, he would roll off the side of the iceberg as soon as another wave crashed into it and would fall into the churning current below. Even worse, he could be crushed between two floating icebergs. Or if he were to hold on after sticking the landing, but slip even slightly, he could get his leg caught and snapped off. But before he could jump, he'd have to leverage himself out of the water, which was no small feat in itself.

Larry threw his longboard on top of the landlocked iceberg and began pulling himself on top of the ice. As he struggled up the ice, the edge broke loose, dropping him back into the water. He lifted himself up again, but the shelf broke off, plopping him into the water. For the next twenty minutes, he kept prying himself out of the water, knowing at some point he'd find a chunk of ice that would support his weight. As the snot-filled icicles formed under his nose, Larry knew conditions would only grow colder.

Finally, he managed to scale the iceberg and scramble over it toward safety. He was able to make it out of the lake, but by then he was utterly exhausted and feared he wouldn't be able to make the twenty-yard walk to his truck. As hypothermia set in, he was losing the use of his arms and legs. Pausing to catch his breath on the ice-covered beach was not an option. He ran as fast as he could—looking like a charging rhino with a broken leg—but when he reached the truck his hands were too cold to grip his keys. "Am I going to freeze to death while standing outside my car?" he said to himself.

He saw the barren square of pavement where Mark's truck had been parked not long ago and felt truly alone in his predicament. Growing desperate, he considered putting the key in his mouth, knowing it would freeze to his lips and probably break off some teeth but would warm up enough to turn the lock.

Despite the hypothermia impeding his thought process, Larry chose, instead, to balance his car key between the fingers of his ice-covered gloves. He lunged forward toward the door lock, puncturing the thin layer of ice covering it, and using his entire body weight to shift open the lock, he heard a click—open! He jumped inside the truck and blasted the heat. As his fingertips tingled with the return of blood flow, he grasped the gearshift, ground the truck into drive, and bolted home.

Once again a Williams twin had survived a brush with death. Although a warm shower helped thaw him out that afternoon, the painful shivering attacks he suffered throughout the spring were an unmistakable reminder of what he had put his body through at the start of the year.

That same summer, Mitch also began suffering from inexplicable surges of pain. Always active and a regular at aerobics, she grew frustrated when a nagging ache slowed her down. Originally diagnosed with a pulled muscle in her lower back, Mitch assumed the source of the pain came from doing too much housework, lifting a heavy pot roast out of the oven, or cleaning the garage with Lee a few weeks earlier. Despite doctors prescribing a cocktail of pain medications, her symptoms would only subside for a couple of weeks before her dosage needed to be increased. As the school year progressed at Farnsworth Middle School, Mitch kept teaching her English as a Second Language classes despite excruciating bouts of pain. She knew something wasn't right, but as the family matriarch, she had to stay strong and keep her household stable.

"We'll battle through this together," she reassured Lee and Trevor. "We always have." Her bold statement had twenty-six years of a solid marriage behind it. Mitch and Lee's relationship had been based on trust. Her subtle sense of humor was the perfect complement to Lee's over-the-top shenanigans. It seemed her sarcasm was the only way she could express her frustrations with the intensifying pain. "It'll take more than straw to break this camel's back," she said through gritted teeth.

Lee worried about her deteriorating condition, and his anxiety led to a renewed obsession with his lawn, which is where Larry found him on a humid evening in July a year after Mitch's initial diagnosis.

"I need your help," Larry said. "I just got a call from John-Paul Beeghly, who said he was making a new *Endless Summer*."

"What surf cameraman isn't?" Lee said sarcastically. "They all think they're making the next great surf movie."

"No," Larry said. "They're actually filming the new *Endless Summer*, and Bruce Brown's son Dana is directing it."

"I don't know if I want to get involved in something like that," Lee said, "especially since Mitch hasn't been feeling well lately."

Knowing how *Endless Summer* introduced the cult of surfing to a worldwide audience back in the sixties, Larry wasn't willing to accept anything less than a yes from his brother. "This could be the biggest thing to ever happen to Great Lakes surfing," Larry said. "We're always looking to be treated legitimately here, and having them come to Sheboygan during this year's Surf Classic would really put us on the map!"

Lee thought for a minute or two and then said, "I'll do it, but *you're* dealing with all the production and media requests. I won't have anything to do with that."

Hugging his brother, Larry said, "This has me so stoked!"

For the next month, Larry's enthusiasm fueled the Surf Classic's preparations. He kept in touch with Beeghly on a weekly basis to ensure the film crew would have the finest accommodations available upon their arrival. He went as far as calling all his friends around the Great Lakes to guarantee a good turnout for the event.

"We can't call Sheboygan the Malibu of the Midwest without crowds," he told them.

On the Wednesday afternoon before the Labor Day weekend, Larry received a phone call to confirm the film crew would be arriving the next day to begin preproduction. "Since your brother Lee is working, we can do that initial meeting without him," John-Paul told Larry. "You can just fill him in on the details."

For the next twenty-four hours, Larry was on edge, fretting over every detail of that year's Surf Classic. "I can't handle this anymore," he told Kerry. "I'm going to the beach."

Larry headed toward the lakefront with his surfboard under one arm and his two dogs—a two-hundred-and-forty-pound

English mastiff and a black Lab—leashed into his other hand. After pulling a bottle of shampoo from the back pocket of his baggy khaki shorts, Larry gave the dogs a thorough scrub before letting them swim around and rinse off in the four-foot waves. Tempted by the seventy-degree water temperature, he threw his surfboard into the water and rode the waves for the next hour. As the sun dipped low in the western sky, he headed home, feeling relaxed and revitalized. Just as he walked through the door, Kerry informed him the film crew was only minutes away.

When Dana Brown arrived with his production team, Larry felt dizzy with excitement—the son of surfing's most legendary filmmaker was walking through his kitchen. When Dana noticed a rare photograph of Greg Noll's Big Wave Team on the wall, he looked at Larry and said, "You know, my dad, Bruce, is at home right now with Greg. They're probably sitting on my front porch having beers as we speak."

After punching a number into his speed-dial, Dana handed his cell phone to Larry, who was nearly speechless. It was one of the most surreal conversations of his life. While legendary filmmaker Bruce Brown and one of his biggest childhood idols, Greg Noll, asked questions about the Sheboygan surf scene, Larry's heart thrashed in his chest. Managing little more than "uh-huh" and "yup," Larry couldn't believe he was talking to two of the greatest surfing legends of all time while he stood in his kitchen. As soon as the conversation ended, he handed the phone to Dana and asked, "Why'd you decide to come here?"

"We thought it would be great to put on the movie poster," Dana joked. "Surfing from Australia to Sheboygan."

Actually, the Wisconsin community wasn't on Dana Brown's preliminary destination list when he started researching surfing locales for his documentary film, *Step into Liquid*. Looking to expand on his father's epic film while also putting a spotlight on the cutting-edge style of twenty-first-century surfing, Dana sought places not on the typical surfing map. He asked the editor of *Surfer Magazine*, Sam George, for places where a surfer's dedication to the sport was as extreme as the conditions they surfed. Sam suggested Sheboygan. Immediately fascinated, Dana researched the city's potential as a featured location for the movie. Soon after that decision, Larry received the call from Dana's producer, John-Paul Beeghly.

Since the winds were bending tree branches against Larry's kitchen window, Dana hoped for a good weekend of surfing. "Tell me more about what exactly is going on tomorrow with the Dairyland Surf Classic," he asked. "When does the competition start?"

"There's not a competition," Larry replied.

"What do you mean?"

"We're not really big into the whole competitive side of surfing," Larry continued. "If the surf's good, nobody will want to get out of the water to compete and none of the judges would get off their boards long enough to score a heat."

"So people come from all over—California, New York, Canada, everywhere—without the promise of any sort of surfing competition?"

Larry nodded. "Since they don't want to surf in a competition, there's no competition."

Dana's eyes widened. "That is so cool! I love it!"

The filmmaker turned to his crew with a smile. "We've come to a place where the stoke of surfing outweighs any sort of competitiveness!"

For the next hour, the production team briefed Larry on what they hoped to accomplish over the next five days of shooting. Then Dana pulled a VHS tape from a large manila envelope and loaded it into Larry's VCR.

The screen came alive with vibrant colors popping out from scenes shot at some of the crew's previous locations. Sitting alongside Dana, John-Paul, and the handful of crewmembers sprawled around his living room, Larry didn't know if he was sitting on the couch or floating above it while being hypnotized by the gorgeous footage. For the next hour, he was transfixed by the lush, green jungles featured in the clip of an American veteran who returned to Southeast Asia for the first time since the war ended, only to leave his surfboard behind for Vietnamese surfers. His jaw dropped when surfers in Texas rode the wakes of one-thousand-foot freighters motoring through the turquoise waters of Galveston Bay. It wasn't until the tape went to black that Larry returned to reality.

"Our signature shot for each segment is a sunrise," Dana told Larry. "So we need you to meet us at the North Point Pier for that first shot of the day no later than five a.m."

When the crew headed back to their hotel for the night, Larry called Lee to explain about being at the beach for the most unusual Dawn Patrol of their lives. "They're a good group of guys," Larry said. "So be sure to make a good impression you meet them."

The next morning, Larry arrived not a minute past five. He saw the massive tripod and camera set up near the North Point Pier. Before the crew turned around to capture their signature shot of a Lake Michigan sunrise, they were taking pictures of some lounging Canadian geese through a thatch of cattail reeds. Hoping to startle them into the air, Dana threw a rock in their direction. The timing couldn't have been more perfect for Lee, who decided to march straight up to them with a disgusted expression plastered on his face.

"You know, it's illegal in Wisconsin to harass Canada geese," he said sternly. "That's a five-hundred-dollar fine per bird. I have no choice but to arrest you."

The film crew looked at him in stunned silence, completely unaware who he was.

"As long as I've been with the Wisconsin Department of Natural Resources," Lee continued, "I've made a career of putting away thoughtless clowns like you who abuse these poor, innocent birds as nothing more than target fodder."

Believing every word, Dana Brown stammered, "We're sorry. We just wanted to grab a shot for our film."

As Lee finished counting how many geese were scrambling into the sky, he extended his right hand toward the filmmaker. "By the way, I'm Lee Williams. It's a pleasure to meet you."

That greeting set the tone for the remainder of the weekend. Lee and Larry did their best to keep up the witty banter and practical jokes, which relaxed the crew. The filmmakers followed the brothers around as they set up the various events of the day. While organizing the Dairyland Surf Classic's giant paddling race that afternoon—the only "competition" at the Classic, and one that was more for entertainment than serious rivalry—Larry was unable to command the large, uncooperative crowd with his bullhorn. With the film crew rolling, it seemed every bodyboarder, windboarder, and paddleboarder who lived on the Great Lakes wanted in on the race. Whenever Larry tried explaining the rules through his bullhorn, he had to threaten to use the aerosol air horn in his other hand if the crowd didn't settle down. The only person who seemed to be paying attention was Otto, the crew' audio mixer, who captured all the film's sounds through an orb-shaped, fur-covered microphone at the end of a fifteen-foot aluminum boom pole.

Out of the corner of his eye, Larry saw the fuzzy mop-top covering the microphone and decided to defuse his frustration by spinning around and grabbing hold of it. With a mischievous grin, he held the aerosol horn tightly against the fur-covered blimp, acting as if he were about to press his finger on the trigger. Otto jerked the boom pole as hard as he could, propelling Larry through the air toward him. Just as Larry was about to crash into the digital audio mixer, Otto hit him square in the chest with the palm of his hand, flattening Larry backward onto the sand, knocking the smirk off his face. The otherwise passive sound mixer screamed, "What were you thinking? You could have killed me! You could have blown out my eardrums!"

"Sorry, man. I was just kidding," Larry said. As Otto chastised him, Larry heard someone laughing behind him. It was Lee.

"I can just see the headphones exploding and brains squirting out of the guy's nose," Lee giggled.

The incident blew over as Dana focused the crew on capturing surfers in the water. Much to the crew's delight, there was some small surf at North Point during that first day of filming. With everybody in the water hoping to get into the film, Lee and Larry seemed to be the only two standing on land. When Dana asked why they weren't in the water, Lee explained, "We've got too much going on with getting the Dairyland organized and all."

"Well, we need some footage of you and your brother paddling out together and surfing a few waves," Dana said. "So you have to go out there since that's the whole reason the cameras are here."

Lee and Larry reluctantly grabbed their boards and headed into the water. After surfing two waves, they returned to the shore, refusing to go back out. "It just isn't worth it," Larry commented, knowing their attempts to ride the small surf would come back to haunt them. "If you film us surfing these small waves, everyone will think Sheboygan is a fraud."

"Speaking of frauds, what's with *that* guy?" Dana asked as he pointed toward the only guy surfing without a wetsuit and leash.

"He's the local kook," Larry said, gritting his teeth in embarrassment. *Kook* is a term used by surfers to describe a fool lacking any sort of etiquette on a board. "Every beach has at least one."

"Fortunately, they make for good entertainment," Dana declared.

Lee and Larry seethed as the kook began a clumsy attempt at cross-stepping across the board toward its nose. It was so sloppy and amateurish, Dana told his cinematographer, "Turn the camera on this clown!"

When the camera turned on him, the kook fell off his board almost on cue. His leash-less surfboard washed toward North Point's rocky shoreline. When the board began crashing against the protruding rocks near shore, the kook swam toward it, refusing to ask anyone for help.

"He probably doesn't want this on film," Lee said to Dana.

When a young surfer shouted, "His board is going to be ruined. I'm going to go get it," Larry grabbed the teenager by the shirt.

"Listen, kid," Larry said. "If he wants to showboat like that for the camera—surfing without a wetsuit and leash, trying to pull off every move in the book—you leave him be. That's the surfer's code when dealing with a kook."

The kid looked at Larry and smiled. "Yup, you're right."

As the board continued banging around the rocks, spectators stood watching with their arms folded. When the kook retrieved it and approached the shore, he began grunting loudly in hopes somebody would notice him, but the crowd didn't budge. That's when Larry turned back toward the kid and said, "The idiot could've asked for help, but knowing him, he would've thought that was some sort of compromise on his dignity." As the kook stood alone with his broken board, Larry said, "That's a well-earned comeuppance when you're a knucklehead surfer."

When the sun set on the first day of the 2000 Dairyland Surf Classic, the party moved from the sand to the local bars. The party lasted into the early morning. When Dana stumbled out of a tavern at three in the morning, he said to Larry, "Five o'clock tomorrow morning at North Point. See you there."

After an hour and a half of sleep, Lee and Larry met Dana and his crew next to the South Pier lighthouse. As soon as the sun peeked out over the horizon, Dana began the interview with Larry, but he wasn't happy with how things looked. "Please face the sun," he told Larry. "And take off your sunglasses. We want to see your eyes."

When the sun's rays pierced his bloodshot eyes, Larry looked like Popeye—squinting eyes and puffy face from a heavy night of drinking.

When asked a question, he was only able to answer in a scratchy mumble.

"I'll be surprised if anybody recognizes me in this," he joked.

As soon as Larry regained his voice, Dana focused his interview on how Wisconsin surfers didn't resemble the dudes who "hang ten" in California or Hawaii. To further emphasize his point, he wanted the quintessential image that would combine the worlds of Wisconsin and surfing. "Do you know any farmers around here?" Dana asked.

"Not really," Larry replied.

"How can you not know any farmers?" Dana asked. "This is Wisconsin and you've lived here all your life."

"We live in town," Lee snapped.

"Let's say we drive ten miles outside of town," Larry said. "We should be able to find a farmer willing to cooperate."

The brothers headed out in Lee's car in search of a farm while the film crew followed in their production van. Driving through the lush topography of rolling green hills, the caravan passed by Kohler's renowned Whistling Straits Golf Course, where the cinematographer decided to hang the camera out the window to capture Lee's little red Honda Civic driving along the countryside with the surfboard strapped to the roof. It was the shot Dana hoped for and would open the Sheboygan segment of *Step into Liquid*.

When Dana found a farm with a view of Lake Michigan, he asked the Williams brothers if they could get permission to shoot in the field.

"Most farmers are friendly, but they don't like being hassled in the morning," Lee said. "They're too busy milking cows."

"I've got confidence you boys can convince him," Dana replied. "You're both naturally charming."

When Lee and Larry walked into the milk shed in search of the farmer, they were overcome by the stench of manure and spoiled milk. They passed nearly two hundred head of dairy cows aligned in milking stalls before finding a farmhand who told them the boss was out back. Following the sound of a constant stream of cussing, Lee and Larry found the farm's owner tending to a cow hooked up to a broken milker.

"Hi," Larry greeted the frustrated farmer. "We're making a movie and were hoping you wouldn't mind if we walk out into your pasture and—"

"Yeah, no problem," the farmer said without looking up. He didn't want to know anything about the film, what the crew wanted to do on his property, or if he could be in it. He was preoccupied with trying to milk his cow. "Wisconsin hospitality," Dana exclaimed. As the crew stood at the edge of the pasture, a trio of cows, each chewing on a cud, looked at them from behind a round hay bale.

"We can't film those round hay bales," Lee told Dana. "They've been outlawed."

"Really, why's that?" Dana played along.

"Because the cows weren't getting a square meal!" Lee laughed as the film crew offered a courtesy chuckle.

Dana, being the good sport, smiled and turned to the Williams brothers. "Okay, you two. Take off your shoes and walk toward the cows. And take your surfboards along."

Reluctantly trudging through the field dotted with fresh cow pies, they were approached by a couple of inquisitive cows. Even though Sheboygan is no sprawling metropolis, Lee and Larry were very much city kids and weren't quite sure what to make of their curious onlookers. When a cow started licking Lee's face, he needed reassurance. "Are you sure they're vegetarians?"

Soon, more cows approached, attracted by the surfboard. As a dozen cows crowded around Lee and Larry, Dana said, "In your lifetime, did you ever imagine you'd be with the guys from *The Endless Summer* standing in manure as cows lick you?"

"It doesn't get more surreal than this," Larry said, realizing the entire group was experiencing one of those moments in life that would never be forgotten.

By that afternoon, the skies grew overcast and the temperatures cooled as tea-colored waves rolled onto shore. Dropping their clipboards and Dairyland Surf Classic responsibilities in the process, Lee and Larry jumped on their boards so Dana could get some good footage of them surfing. With his board in the soup, Larry had the churning white water snapping at his ankles while turning out of waves just as they broke up. Lee was able to slide along the foaming edge of the cresting waves, twisting and arching his body to compensate for the radical changes in wave speed as he approached the shoreline. Despite a handful of good runs, Lee and Larry could sense Dana's disappointment in not being able to film better surfing conditions. With no storm systems due overnight, Dana feared his Labor Day shoot would be a bust. "What if there are no waves tomorrow?" he asked. "What happens then?"

"Are you kidding?" Lee reassured him. "Like my brother always says, who doesn't love spending a day at the beach?"

"The Dairyland isn't about the surf," Larry added. "It's about good times with good friends."

Following the annual potluck dinner, a musical act took the stage. Dana and his crew reveled in the camaraderie. Beer flowed out of kegs while the dance floor filled with raucous partiers. Hands waved in the air as swaying beer washed over the rims of plastic cups, refreshing the crowd below. Just as someone broke a table in half and another started crushing beer cans in his biceps, Dana walked up to Lee and Larry, who were enjoying the scene from outside the mosh pit.

"This is a ripper party," Dana said. "Now I understand why everyone is so dedicated to the surf scene here. This is outrageous!"

"Wait until the second band gets on stage," Larry baited.

With two bands taking turns rocking out on stage, the crowd overflowed into the bar's sand volleyball court, quickly turning the Dairyland Surf Classic into a Sheboygan block party. The surrounding sandpit, sidewalk, and parking lot looked as if a tornado had blown through as broken bottles, glasses, paper plates, underwear, shirts, pants, shoes, and beer cans were strewn in every direction. Leaning against the bar, Lee and Larry could only smile as their party engrossed even the most pessimistic of the crew members.

"How are you guys going to top this?" Dana asked.

"Next year we're reuniting the Beatles to cover Beach Boys tunes," Lee said.

By Sunday morning, even after polishing off a jumbo-size bottle of aspirin, Larry was still hung over and burnt out. When he didn't show up for the first shot at five o'clock, the crew sent a production assistant to his house to get him.

"Tell them you couldn't find me," Larry told the kid.

The kid obliged. Larry was crashed out on the couch with a cold compress melting on his forehead. An hour later, the production assistant returned, cautiously knocking on the door. "Mr. Williams," he called. "Mr. Williams, they need you down at the beach."

Rousing himself from his fermented haze, Larry cracked the front door with a frown on his face. The kid looked at him with a nervous smile. "They won't let me return without you."

"Listen, sport," Larry grunted. "Five straight days of drinking, screaming, yelling, and getting only three hours of sleep has finally caught up with me. Just tell them I wasn't home."

Back on the beach, the waves were cooperative but not awe-inspiring. Lee and a handful of friends, all dressed in their trademark black wetsuits, settled into a surfing cycle, taking turns getting atop waves and not talking much while paddling out. The huge Sheboygan waves Dana sought to capture on film would not arrive during his visit, forcing him to settle for several sets of reasonably clean four-footers. As the mid-afternoon sun ducked behind the clouds, all of the surfers were exhausted. Waiting for his last ride, Lee noticed a shimmering, silver-smooth wave approaching. He hoisted onto his board and drifted with a warm breeze across the water's surface, soaring across the water for a hundred yards on a five-foot wall he could barely see in his peripheral vision. Pulling onto shore, Lee tucked his surfboard under his arm, walked up to Dana, and said, "Sheboygan is a pretty great place with decent surf. I'm thinking of moving here."

About an hour later, a ringing phone roused Larry from sleep. Lee told him, "We're done filming, so you can come out of your social coma now."

After driving to the American Club's Horse & Plow in Kohler for the crew's wrap dinner, Larry found himself sitting next to his brother, absorbing the last few surreal moments of his weekend with Dana Brown. With everyone worn out from five days of shooting, the dinner was subdued but pleasant. When it was time to go, the director and his crew loaded into their minivan, barely wedging themselves into the spaces not occupied by gear and suitcases packed to the ceiling. As they drove away, Larry told

Lee, "We've done a lot together, including being born, but this has to be pretty high on our list of highlights."

"Yeah," Lee said. "But it would've been better if our wave machine hadn't been in the repair shop."

That winter, Lee and Larry surfed whenever the weather cooperated with their busy schedules. Early mornings worked best. Their jobs allowed them to continue surfing on their hometown beach as they approached age fifty. When accused by co-workers of having Peter Pan complexes, they would explain how their interest in surfing was no different from jogging, restoring antique cars, or re-enacting Civil War battles.

Surfing that winter also served as Lee's escape from Mitch's growing discomfort in her back. Her pain had grown so severe she could barely function without extensive medication. Sitting in a car, walking to the mailbox, and pushing a shopping cart became torturous. After six months of adhering to the doctor's prescriptions, physical therapy, and regular visits to the chiropractor, she felt her symptoms were only worsening. By the spring of 2001, she insisted on getting a fresh diagnosis.

While she waited to receive the results of her CT scan at Sheboygan's Memorial Hospital, Lee and Trevor sat with her. When they ventured down the hallway to buy her a soda, they overheard a couple of doctors discussing her condition. At first, they refused to believe what they were hearing, but when they both saw the X-ray the doctors held up to the light, their fears were confirmed. But by the time they returned to her room, Mitch had already received the news from the doctors—she had cancer, a malignant tumor on her spinal column.

Chapter Nine

All Mitch could do was sob. As she lay in the hospital bed, Lee approached her and rested his head in her lap. "How could they have missed it all this time?" he said, forcing back tears. "I just don't understand."

"That's not important," she said, wiping away her tears. "We need to focus on the now." Lee and Trevor stood next to her, admiring her strength. "They're admitting me to St. Luke's Hospital in Milwaukee for immediate treatment."

That evening, Larry drove straight to the hospital after work. Although the message Lee had left for him didn't sound urgent, it was obvious their plans of spending another night downing a few beers, sharing some laughs, and watching one of their favorite surfers, Gerry Lopez, in their favorite movie, *Big Wednesday*, would be postponed. When Larry stepped into Mitch's hospital room, he realized something wasn't right. The bed was empty, and Lee was sitting on a small chair in the corner. Larry cautiously approached. He said, "Hey, bro."

Lee kept his head down, focusing on a hospital-monogrammed folder filled with numerous cancer treatment pamphlets. "What's up?" Larry asked.

Between a handful of sniffles and sobs, Lee blurted out, "Mitch has a golf ball-sized tumor next to her spinal column. It's inoperable. They're transporting her to Milwaukee right now for further treatment."

"I'm so sorry," Larry replied.

Lee nodded.

Larry said, "This is terrible."

"Well, don't you have something spiteful to say?" Lee said.

"No. She's family and that's what's important," Larry replied. "What can I do to help?"

"Nothing. I don't need anything," Lee said, covering his face with his hands. Knowing his brother was too proud to ask for anything—especially in a moment of need—Larry hugged him, refusing to loosen his grasp even slightly.

"Let's get you washed up," Larry said. "Then I'll drive you down to Milwaukee."

Upon her admittance into the Vince Lombardi Cancer Center, Mitch received a battery of tests to evaluate her health and determine if she was fit enough for the rigorous radiation therapy and chemotherapy that would fight the cancer. As she endured more aggressive courses of treatment, she often found herself coping with high fevers and vomiting. Throughout the long and challenging months, Mitch stayed motivated by focusing on her goal of one day getting back to the beach to see her husband ride the waves.

"I should've spent more time watching you surf," she'd tell Lee. "Your gracefulness on a wave will always be one of my favorite mental images."

Although she was at one of the most prestigious cancer treatment centers in the country, Mitch never felt comfortable around the sterile white walls and tile floors. She insisted that Lee be at her side around the clock, which forced him to abandon all of his other interests and responsibilities.

"I don't care if I lose my house, my job, and everything I own," he said many times. "I will never leave her side."

For the next two months, Lee sat at his wife's bedside, hoping doctors would find a way to operate on the tumor or that the cancer would miraculously disappear. When it was clear to her that the chemotherapy was not helping, Mitch decided she had had enough. "I could go through all the treatment again," she said, "but I can tell from the doctors' faces that there's very little chance of it working and more chance that it will kill me."

She looked at Lee with her emerald eyes bloodshot from the days, weeks, and months of crying. In a soft voice, she said, "I want to go home."

"But you have the best care here," Lee told her.

"I want to be with the people who I love and who love me. This hospital will never be home."

That next morning, Mitch was discharged from the Vince Lombardi Cancer Center. With Lee behind the wheel, they took the scenic route north back to Sheboygan. Driving along the Lake Michigan shoreline, the glistening waves were never out of her sight as the wind off the lake whipped across her face. "This is the freshest air I've ever breathed," she told him.

Arriving home, Mitch found her makeshift hospital room already incorporated into the living room. The sterile white bed linens, stainless steel bed frame, and handful of medical instruments contrasted the otherwise warm living space she had enjoyed for so many years. But all Mitch cared about was eating food out of her refrigerator, looking out her front window, and sleeping under her own roof.

Although able to enjoy the comforts of home, she still required constant care when not receiving chemotherapy at the hospital. When her tumor grew so large it paralyzed her from the waist down, Lee never left her side, continuing to miss extensive amounts of work, refusing invitations to hang out with friends, and only leaving the house for groceries or medicine. Since Trevor was away at college, whenever Lee had to leave for a mandatory meeting under the threat of losing his job, Larry would come to the house and stay with Mitch.

Even in her deteriorating state, their relationship was chilly at best, but that didn't mean he didn't care about her. Often sitting on his brother's front porch with a monitor in his hand, Larry would listen and wait to help whenever Mitch called for assistance. While watching people around the neighborhood mow their lawns, walk their dogs, and play baseball in the street, he was beside himself. "Does anybody realize what's going on in this house? There's someone dying in here. Isn't the world supposed to stop?"

As weeks transformed into months, Larry continued to support them any way he could, knowing how much Mitch meant to the Williams family. Since he was the only person Lee felt comfortable talking with, he would grab a twelve-pack of beer and a handful of surf movies before coming to the house, allowing his brother an opportunity to catch up on life and escape, if only for a few hours, from the nightmare that consumed him. On the nights Lee struggled to fall asleep, Larry would sit next to him on the couch. When Lee finally did sleep, Larry listened to the monitor in case Mitch woke up.

When Lee started suffering panic attacks, he began working more hours at the grocery store. That left Larry to run more errands, bringing back groceries or picking up specialized medical linens from the laundry service. Since he was spending more time with Mitch, often heading straight to the house after work, they decided to shove aside years of disagreements and soon found the humor in their years of squabbles. While talking about the future, they both knew how much they needed each other—if not for each other, then for Lee and Trevor. "The saddest thing is that I won't be able to watch my family grow old," she'd tell Larry. "Nothing made me happier than watching my boys smile."

Mitch knew her body was succumbing to the cancer, but she refused to let it compromise her spirit. While watching Lee prepare her daily chemical concoction of painkillers, she decided she wanted to do something fun during her Friday night alone with her husband. "Hon," she said, "I want to watch you surf again."

"It's dark out," he said. "Plus, how are we going to get you to the beach?"

She shook her head. "No. I want to watch you surf when you were young. When you were the man I fell in love with."

Lee paused, wiping a tear from his eye. Setting down the bottle in his hand, he walked over to the bookcase. Finding a VHS tape labeled with nothing more than a title scribbled in magic marker over a torn-off piece of masking tape, he placed it into the VCR and pressed the play button. Turning the television so Mitch could see the entire screen, he sat next to her as they watched his old Super 8 surfing films from 1968. As he gently held her hand, he wished the night would go on forever.

Michele Williams died on June 20, 2001. She was forty-eight.

The visitation room at the funeral parlor was alive with color from numerous floral bouquets and dozens of enlarged personal photos of a young and vibrant Mitch—each as spectacular as the next. While assembling the visual love letter to celebrate his beloved wife's life, Lee made the pictures even more powerful and poignant when he read the eulogy, which he wrote in her words. Anyone listening to it would've thought she had written it herself as she proceeded to thank all the people who had come into her life and to share how much they each meant to her. At the end of the service, Lee stood tall, staying composed as a long line of people offered him condolences. The entire time, he did not cry as attendees shared their favorite memories of Mitch.

Walking up to his brother, Larry reached out and pulled him in for a hug. When Lee let out one long howling sob that echoed throughout the entire funeral home, he at last revealed the amount of sorrow he felt. It was a display of pain Lee would never show again in public. He had to be strong and carry on, if not for himself, then for Trevor.

Following Mitch's funeral, Lee began working long hours at the grocery store, trying to redirect his grief. The thought of being alone with his thoughts was terrifying, so there wasn't an over-time shift he wouldn't offer to cover. "There's nothing for me to go home to," he'd tell his boss. Spending nearly one hundred hours a week at the store, he made sure to be working straight through the Fourth of July weekend, refusing to even acknowledge it as a holiday. He even stopped returning calls from Larry, who was reluctantly organizing the upcoming Surf Classic on his own. Lee exchanged every free moment in his life for more hours of stocking shelves and displaying produce until his brother showed up at the grocery store toward the end of July.

Confronting Lee with their mutual responsibilities regarding the upcoming surf event, he said, "Look, I need your help. Kerry is pregnant, and I can't pull the Dairyland together by myself."

"Kerry's pregnant? Are you sure it's yours?" Lee joked. "You know you're pushing fifty."

"Oh yeah, it's mine," the future papa bragged. "Kerry says the baby is already doing barrel rolls in her tummy. Definitely a surfer."

Lee felt happy for the first time in months. "Well, I guess cutting back my schedule here to help you with the Dairyland might be a good idea," Lee said. "It probably wouldn't hurt if I found my way back into the water as well."

Lee started spending more time at Larry's house coordinating the upcoming Labor Day event. It served as the perfect distraction for the grieving widower as they sat at the kitchen table less than a week before the Dairyland Surf Classic's kickoff.

"Have we contacted the Sheboygan Board of Tourism yet?" Larry asked, going through the final checklist to see what had yet to be done.

Lee nodded. "And the Wisconsin Board of Tourism too," he added.

Both were aware of the looming irony. The surfing journey they had been on through the past forty years had begun arcing into a full circle. The respect they craved from their hometown as rebellious, adolescent surfers willing to push the limits of society's patience in the sixties had manifested itself into a working relationship with the mayor, local politicians, and the Sheboygan Chamber of Commerce, who now helped to promote the positive aspects of surfing. Public safety officials asked for their help when addressing the rip currents and pier safety problems that, like many communities along the Great Lakes, plagued Sheboygan. With the cooperation of civic, state, and federal officials, the Williams brothers helped develop and place water safety signage around all of Sheboygan's most populated waterways.

Despite the numerous posted warnings about the treacherous rip currents and other Lake Michigan water hazards, a young boy playing in waist-high water was pulled out into open waters, drowning as a result of a rip current. Following the boy's funeral, the mayor asked Lee and Larry if they could help bring further awareness to the city's drowning-prevention program. For them, it was an opportunity to give back to a community and the natural resource they had loved all their lives. Larry, never one to shy away from a large crowd, began speaking at schools about the dangers of swimming alone. Lee spent his free weekends filling out grant applications so even more signs could be posted along the shoreline about the dangers of rip currents.

Knowing they wouldn't have many free moments in the upcoming week with all that had yet to be coordinated for the Surf Classic, Larry set down his pen and said to Lee, "Let's go for a surf."

Paddling out together, the Williams brothers straddled their boards as a set of six- to eight-foot waves rolled in. Positioned nearly fifty yards beyond the Elbow, Lee anticipated the arrival of the next big wave while noticing an out-of-towner to his left. As the wave began to curl, Lee took it on, balancing himself just outside the impact zone. Realizing the out-of-towner was about to pass underneath him, he pulled up the nose of his board as the wave passed. The maneuver left Lee exposed as the top of the wave pitched him, catapulting him down the growling wave. While somersaulting down, drilling deeper under the water, he watched his wetsuit boots flip past. Just as he was about to surface, his board spanked him on the head. Scrambling for his board, he was able to clear his eyes long enough to see the second wave in the set smack him with the clout of a European bullet train.

Unable to surface, Lee was now drinking Lake Michigan instead of breathing air. Despite the adrenaline pumping through his veins, he couldn't orient himself between the surface and lake bottom. Drilled by another wave, despite still being submerged, Lee somersaulted again, sensing he was even farther from the surface as everything got darker.

Out of desperation, he stopped struggling and let his body go limp, letting gravity show him the way. As he sank toward the soft Sheboygan Bay sand, he flailed his arms and legs trying to find the surface. When his head popped out of the water, Larry was almost on top of him, still straddling his board.

"Looks like you took a little beating," Larry said with a smile. "Lake Michigan sure knew how to welcome you back."

Lee couldn't speak, coughing and spitting out as much lake water as he could. Riding the next wave into shore on his broken surfboard, Lee was soon joined by his brother. "Mother Nature sure knows how to put us in our place," Larry declared. "Of course, only the good die young."

"Yeah, and those sixteen minutes I've got on you just saved my life," Lee chimed.

As they took a moment for Lee to catch his breath and assess the damage to his surfboard, Larry said, "It's nice to have you back, bro."

"It's good to be back," Lee replied.

That would be the last time Lee and Larry had an opportunity to put their feet in the water as they spent the next week working an intense schedule of radio, television, and newspaper interviews while planning and coordinating the final details of the Surf Classic.

And their hard work paid off. Everyone agreed the 2001 Dairyland Surf Classic was the best one yet. The Saturday afternoon paddleboard competitions were decided by highly contested photo finishes, the skies were blue, the eighty-degree temperature was humidity-free, and the warm breeze blew away all the pesky mosquitoes. And, of course, there was plenty of cold beer to go around.

Following the annual potluck dinner that night, the brothers gathered around a bright and snapping bonfire in Larry's backyard with their group of surfing friends, all of whom tried to give Lee a little extra support in light of what he had lost in the past year.

"Where's that broken-down surfboard of yours?" Lester Priday asked in his thick Australian accent. "I've got a great way to fix it up. Nothing a pyre of flames can't solve."

"The board's still salvageable," Lee replied. "Plus, I can't afford to buy a new one."

The burning of Lee's prized surfboard

Lee's lack of cooperation prompted Lester to pull the surfboard from behind the picnic bench he was sitting on. The group of slightly intoxicated men began chanting, "Burn it! Burn it! Burn it!"

"Calm them down," Lee told Larry. "They can't take my board away from me."

"It's not fixable," Larry said.

"Yes it is," Lee barked.

Knowing his brother was as frugal as he was stubborn, Larry tried flattery: "You really deserve a new board. Not some outdated, chipped clunker."

Larry turned to Lester, looking for some sort of acknowledgment. Lester turned to Lee, then at the board and back at Lee. "Let's burn it, mate!"

"If it'll make you happy," Lee mustered as he finished his beer.

As the board was passed over the crowd toward the bonfire, Lee watched his fiberglass companion receive a burial fitting a fallen Viking hero, except instead of being cremated at sea, the board met its fate in the middle of a Sheboygan subdivision.

Lunging the surfboard onto the crest of the burning bonfire, Lester shouted at the top of his lungs, "To new beginnings!"

The group cheered, "To new beginnings!"

Lee knew it was time to embrace the technology offered to surfers today. He browsed surfboard suppliers from around the globe via the Internet and realized how far the retail merchandising of surfing had evolved since he had purchased his first shellacked piece of ten-foot-long marine plywood out of a Sheboygan garage for twenty-five dollars. He could not only find a state-of-the-art shortboard that featured an improved rail curve, tail design, and bottom contour, but also view all 360 degrees of the board before purchasing it—a far cry from the grainy, black-and-white mail-order forms shoehorned into the back pages of those 1960s surfing magazines.

The Internet also gave Lee and Larry the opportunity to post an invitation to the upcoming 2002 Dairyland Surf Classic on the Sheboygan Chamber of Commerce's Web site and to send out emails to all their friends about the weekend's schedule. One announcement that wasn't included concerned the newest addition to the Sheboygan surf scene—Larry and Kerry's newborn daughter, Madhury "Mady" Lake Williams, whose name was inspired by the Sanskrit word for "sweet." Between her dad and uncle, everyone knew it would be only a matter of time before she was fitted for her first wetsuit and balanced atop her first surfboard, most likely within days of taking her first steps. As Larry and Kerry passed Mady to her proud uncle and cousin, Lee and Trevor, she cooed and gurgled on cue, bringing joy to their hearts, which had been so badly treated in that terrible year. Mady brought hope and laughter and made them feel alive again. For Larry, life had come

Larry, Kerry, and Mady in 2007

full circle. Mady's birth reminded him how precious life was and how blessed he was to have a second chance at parenthood—a chance he looked forward to taking again.

The next summer, in August 2003, *Step into Liquid* was released in theaters across the United States. Immediately embraced by the surfing community, the film premiered in subsequent months throughout Canada, Asia, and Europe, quickly becoming an international hit. Dana Brown's film captured not only some of the most incredible surfing footage ever brought to the screen, but also captured the intoxicating power surfing has over people's souls. Although many of the world's top professional surfers appeared in the film—including Kelly Slater, Keala Kennelly, Rob Machado, Layne Beachley, and Taj Burrow—theater audiences seemed to connect most with Lee and Larry Williams and their thickly accented Sconnie surfer-speak.

"I can't even begin to count how many of our friends from California and Hawaii walked out of the theater mimicking our pronunciation of *stoked*," Lee told a *Chicago Tribune* reporter.

Since that year's Dairyland Surf Classic was only a couple weeks away, Lee and Larry were bombarded with a larger-than-usual list of media requests, a salute to their new celebrity status. Although they were excited that the film gave Sheboygan credibility among surfers worldwide, they couldn't help but feel a bit disappointed that their segment portrayed them as more tongue-in-cheek than they'd have liked, leaving them to defend some of their comments, which were pulled out of context. "I still stand behind the statement," Larry said defensively to a local television reporter, "that we do have barrels so big you can hide a Volkswagen in them."

When one reporter asked them if they were surfing legends, Lee and Larry realized how the movie had placed them into the pop culture lexicon of surfing. "We're uncomfortable with it, but flattered," Lee admitted.

"When you talk about surfing legends, you've got Duke Kahanamoku, Miki Dora, and Gregg Noll," Larry added. "Then there's Gerry Lopez, the pipeline master himself. How are Larry and Lee Williams mentioned in with those names?"

When asked about their legacy in surfing, Larry paused for a moment. "Giving more than we took," he answered. He mentioned nothing about Lee's closet full of trophies or his own celebrity status as the face of the Dairyland Surf Classic. "The best

Step into Liquid
movie poster
COURTESY
OF EVERETT
COLLECTION

surfers do it all the time," Larry continued. "If you have a good attitude, share your good attitude by sharing a ride or a bar of wax or zipping the back zipper on somebody's wetsuit."

"If you want to define that as our legacy, that's more important to us than ever being considered a legend," Lee concluded.

The acclaim Lee and Larry received from their appearance in *Step into Liquid* made them recognizable even among casual surfing fans. From folks in their neighborhood supermarket to fans in places far from Sheboygan, they had become a viable part of the international surfing scene. Their faces seemed to be everywhere, with everyone from old high school girlfriends and surfing buddies to distant family members reaching out to reconnect with them now that they had become famous.

When Larry's doorbell rang early on a Saturday morning during the summer of 2006, he was a little taken aback when what looked like a teenage boy stood at the door, nervously rubbing his hands together. "Are you Larry Williams?" he asked as his voice cracked.

"Yeah," he replied.

"Great. I've been meaning to do this for a long time." The young man paused just as Larry cut him off.

"You're not going to tell me I'm your father, are you?" Larry asked.

"No. No. No. I'm Aaron Levanduski," he replied with a smile. "I'm one of the boys you saved on the pier fifteen years ago."

Larry was stunned. All he could muster was, "Really!"

The boy nodded. "I saw your picture in the paper because of your movie," he said while becoming visibly choked up. "And I never really thanked you for saving my life."

As the young man's eyes misted, Larry didn't know what to say.

"We'd like to have a barbecue in your honor," Aaron offered. "I'd like you to meet my mom, my grandma, my grandpa, and my wife to be."

"Absolutely," Larry obliged. "It would be an honor."

That weekend, Larry met Aaron's extended family. As they celebrated the anniversary of Larry's rescue efforts on the pier, it became a tearful reunion as family members, one by one, thanked Larry for his unselfish heroics. Making sure to deflect the attention back onto Aaron, he was just happy the kid took advantage of the opportunity to become an upstanding citizen with hopes of venturing off to college. When wrapping his arms around Aaron and his fiancée for a final photograph, Larry felt a sense of peace from knowing he had made a significant difference in somebody's life and that Aaron was making the most of it.

Lee was not recognized as often as Larry but he, too, experienced some surprising encounters. As a volunteer during the 2004 PGA Championship at the nearby Whistling Straits Golf Course, he was tending to the practice green when a gentleman approached him with the all-too-familiar, "Aren't you one of those brothers from *Step into Liquid*?"

Since he was surrounded by the likes of Tiger Woods, Phil Mickelson, and some of the most famous names in golf history, Lee didn't quite know what to think as the man walked directly toward him across the putting green, dodging numerous golf balls. "I've got to get your autograph for my daughter," the man insisted. Lee stepped off the green, trying not to bring attention to himself.

"Can I walk and talk with you?" the man asked, finally identifying himself as the father of a competitive surfer from Virginia Beach.

The two talked for nearly an hour as the man had a long list of questions about surfing in Sheboygan. All the while, Lee kept the putting green well groomed, picking up the occasional wayward golf ball.

"My daughter is going to be so impressed I met you," the father exclaimed as he shook Lee's hand one last time. "This is definitely the highlight of my weekend!"

Since *Step into Liquid* had made them the new faces of freshwater surfing, Lee and Larry were invited by fellow Lake Michigan surfer Vince Deur to participate in his latest documentary film, *Unsalted*. The film captured the heritage and majestic backdrops of surfing on the inland oceans through a combination of beautifully shot contemporary footage and home movies going as far back as the 1960s. For the Williams brothers, *Unsalted* not only reflected their passion for the Great Lakes surfing scene but also became somewhat of a surfing scrapbook since it featured many of their photographs and Super 8 films from their early days of wave riding on Sheboygan's lakefront.

The Lake Shore Surf Club reunited in 2005. Back row, from left to right: Rocky Groh, Randy Grimmer, Chuck Reis (obscured), Tom Ziegler, Andy Sommersberger, Steve Ceskowski, Bill Kuitert, John Rusch, Mark Wente, and Chuck Koehler. Front row, from left to right: Lee Williams, Kevin Groh, and Larry Williams

Another opportunity afforded Lee and Larry as a result of *Step into Liquid* was an invitation to surf several of Southern California's breaks. Since their lifelong friend Kevin Groh had gotten divorced earlier in 2005, the Williams brothers decided it was time to reintroduce him to surfing. Through the years, they had never lost touch with him, but Kevin rarely found his way onto a longboard anymore. His interests had shifted to trapping muskrat, beaver, and raccoons for their pelts as well as to fishing nearly every day. Though an ardent outdoorsman, Kevin had never been farther west than the Dakotas, where he had hunted pheasant, or farther east than Grand Haven, where Lee and Larry had taken him to surfing events. When Kevin's divorce papers were finalized, he decided to accompany the brothers on their surfing trip to California, which all agreed would be the best therapy he could receive.

When Lee and Larry first brought up the idea, Kevin said, "My kids are grown and out of the house. My wife took me for everything I had, and she's not getting another dime. So I'm going to cash out my life insurance policy, take that eight hundred dollars, and go with you."

Having never been on an airplane before, Kevin was awestruck, like a five-year-old with both hands pressed against the window and his nose between his hands. He never took his eyes from the window, watching the scenery pass below, speechless during the entire flight. As the plane flew over the Los Angeles basin before landing at LAX International Airport, Kevin couldn't stop pointing out the famous landmarks. "There's the Hollywood sign. There's the Santa Monica Pier. Isn't that the Capitol Records building?"

From the airport, they drove their rental car north on the Pacific Coast Highway toward Malibu. Kevin looked in wonder at the palm trees whisking by at fifty miles an hour. His enthusiasm was contagious as all three grown men started acting like teenagers again. Within an hour, the three lifelong freshwater surfers were surfing in the Pacific Ocean's salty waves as the marine layer of clouds encroaching over the horizon created another legendary California sunset.

"Are you having fun yet, Gripper?" Larry asked.

"This is a dream," Kevin replied, inhaling another breath of ocean air. The next morning, they ventured down to San Clemente, rented boards, and enjoyed an authentic Pacific Coast "Dawn Patrol." By seven o'clock, their boards were strapped on top of their car, and they headed to San Onofre for breakfast. Following a feast of pancakes, eggs, and avocados, they headed out to catch the ten-foot surf. Not long after they were in the ocean, they noticed schools of fish jumping out of the water all around Kevin. As seagulls swooped down, attacking the airborne fish, Kevin looked in awe at the wildlife bursting around him. The Williams brothers realized something more sinister was brewing underneath their friend.

"Gripper!" they called out to him. "Get out of the water!"

Kevin didn't hear them, consumed by the arcing fish and the seagulls snapping them up.

"Kevin!" Larry finally blasted at the top of his lungs.

Kevin looked over at him. "What?" he shouted back.

"SHARK!" Lee screamed. "They're eating the fish below you. That's why they're jumping. Get out of there!"

Startled, as if out of a trance, Kevin paddled toward Lee and Larry, who stood closer to the shore.

Reaching the brothers, Kevin finally realized what he had just witnessed.

"We ain't in Sheboygan anymore," Lee said.

Kevin, his hair dripping, said, "I've been a fisherman my whole life. I should've known those four-hundred-pound dolphins jumping over the nose of my board weren't welcoming a first-time visitor to these parts."

The rest of their vacation was a lot less harrowing until they were approached at the airport by a burly, tattooed Hawaiian man with black wavy hair. Convinced they were about to get mugged, all three reached to cover their wallets as the stranger walked right up to them.

"Don't I know you guys?" he asked.

The small-town Midwestern boys didn't respond, eyeing the big man suspiciously, ready for some type of con.

"Yeah, you're those *Step into Liquid* surfers from Wisconsin. What are you guys doing here?"

The boys broke into a smile and admitted that, indeed, they were the Sheboygan surfers. The Hawaiian guy said that he, too, was a fan of surfing, and they all chatted for a while, exchanging stories. The guy left feeling he had enjoyed a lucky—and unlikely—celebrity sighting while in Hollywood, one he would take back to the islands with him and one that would leave even his most cynical surfing buddies stoked.

After the guy disappeared into the crowd, Kevin looked at Lee and Larry, hoping they kept their egos in check. "I guess if you do anything long enough, sooner or later you're going to be recognized," Kevin said.

The boys agreed. Always surprised and flattered when they were recognized, they knew that their modicum of fame merely reflected their dedication to a life passion.

Over the next few years, they had many encounters with strangers who recognized them as "those twin brothers from Sheboygan who surf." From nurses seeking autographs at Mady's pediatrician's office to customers at the new Chicago restaurant at which Trevor had been named head chef, people approached them. Nobody realized the extent of their expanding sphere of fame until Larry was contacted by a *Sheboygan Press* newspaper reporter on the eve of the 2007 Dairyland Surf Classic for what he thought was another routine interview.

"I'm not sure how to ask you this question," fumbled the reporter.

"Well, if it's about surfing, I've probably already answered it," Larry said, "since ninety percent of my calls this time of year have something to do with it."

"Okay, great," the reporter said with a sigh of relief. "So you already know about the new surfing movie you and your brother are in."

"We've been in several," Larry said. "Which one would you like to talk about?"

"The one where you're an animated surfing chicken."

The garrulous Larry was struck dumb. What did the guy say? A surfing *chicken*? Was this some kind of a joke?

"The movie's called *Surf's Up*," the reporter continued. "How well do you know the movie?"

"There's a surfing chicken?"

Surf's Up movie
poster COURTESY
OF PHOTOFEST

"I guess you don't know about it then." The reporter proceeded to summarize the computer-animated film's comedic
mockumentary plotline about a teenage penguin named Cody
Maverick who was determined to win the most important surfing
competition in the world.

Larry said he had never heard anything about it.

"It's a parody of classic surfing films—*The Endless Summer,
Riding Giants, North Shore.* The penguins are modeled on famous
surfers like Kelly Slater, Rob Machado, Miki Dora, guys like that."

"Okay," Larry said, saying the word slowly, still wondering if
this reporter was pulling his leg.

The reporter went on to explain that when the writers were developing Cody Maverick's sidekick, they thought it would be fun to make him a chicken. Thus was born Chicken Joe, a long-necked geek from the Midwest. But they were stumped on where exactly he'd be from. Where would a rooster from the Midwest learn to surf?

"That's when one of the writers remembered seeing you and your brother in *Step into Liquid*," the reporter said.

The movie only references Sheboygan twice—when Chicken Joe is interviewed near the beginning of the film and again at the end when all the characters are announced individually. But the wave-riding fowl who surfs Lake Michigan off the Sheboygan shoreline steals every scene he is in. Throughout the film, Chicken Joe is underestimated by the other surfers, but much like the two characters that inspired him, that Midwestern chicken sure can surf.

The movie went on to great success, including an Oscar nomination for Best Animated Feature Film in 2008. Actor Jon Heder, best known for his portrayal of Napoleon Dynamite in the movie of that name, supplied Chicken Joe's voice, sounding nothing at all like Larry or Lee. The brothers loved the film and were happy to supply a model for such a likable character. They were even happier to see surfing catch the attention of a whole new generation. They're grateful, however, that the film, unlike *Step into Liquid*, has not increased their celebrity. They've yet to be stopped in an airport or on the beach by an excited fan exclaiming, "Aren't you the model for Chicken Joe in the movie *Surf's Up*?"

In 2008, the Dairyland Surf Classic celebrated its twentieth anniversary. What began as an excuse to watch surf videos, eat some brats, and lie about how well everybody surfed had grown into a party that drew nearly two hundred surfers, some flying in from

Larry, left, and Lee provide final instructions before the paddleboard competition during the 2008 Dairyland Surf Classic. COURTESY OF WILLIAM POVLETICH

as far away as Hawaii and California. Considered to be the largest gathering of freshwater surfers in the world, the Dairyland Surf Classic had become "the annual gathering of the tribes" with all six major Great Lakes surfing organizations in attendance—the Wagner Surf Club from Cleveland; the Southend Surf Crew from Chicago; the Superior Surf Club from Duluth, Minnesota; the Great Lakes Surfing Association from Grand Haven, Michigan; the Wyldewood Surf Club from Port Colborne, Ontario, Canada; and Sheboygan's Team Blatz.

On the beach, car stereos blared with the timeless surf music of the Beach Boys and Dick Dale. Nearly five hundred beachgoers, news reporters, and curious onlookers weaved between beach cruiser bicycles, board art displays, and impromptu gatherings along the Deland Park shoreline.

Paddleboard competitors prepare for the next heat during the 2008 Dairyland Surf Classic. COURTESY OF WILLIAM POVLETICH

By mid-afternoon, Larry was tasked with marching up and
down Broughton Drive with a megaphone, announcing the start
of the Pro Paddling Race. Once all the contestants were wrangled
up, nearly forty-five minutes after it was scheduled to begin, the
race became a frantic endurance test as a dozen surfers splashed
like madmen toward the white buoy one-eighth of a mile offshore.
As the paddlers made the turn and headed back to shore, fellow
wave rider and local photographer Jim Gardner snapped dozens
of photos of them crashing through waves while attempting to
distance themselves from one another. When the two strongest
racers—with unrivaled athletic builds, coordination and speed—
blew across the sand toward the finish line, Lee turned to an en-
thralled spectator. "That's why you've never seen a fat surfer," he
boasted. "Talk about a full-body workout."

From the handheld streamer paper that served as the finish
line, it was apparent the Dairyland Surf Classic would never be

an event the Elias Sports Bureau monitored closely. Although trophies were awarded for first, second, and third place in four age groups, Lee and Larry would be the first to admit that records and statistics from past years were recorded casually, with some of the names of former winners already lost or forgotten.

While walking along Broughton Drive, the main pedestrian thoroughfare of the Dairyland Surf Classic, Lee and Larry couldn't help but glow with pride about how their modest Labor Day weekend surf party had evolved, much like the beachfront that hosted it. The overgrown scrub brush and footpath that once rutted in the shoulder-high grass had been replaced with stairwells and landscaped lawns. The piles of rotting driftwood had been cleared away to make room for playgrounds and bathrooms.

As they made their way along the various vendor booths, which featured everything from jewelry and wooden tiki statues to designer wetsuits and custom surfboards, the Williams brothers made sure to say hello to everyone who had traveled the many miles and hours to attend. It was the least they could do after watching their friends fall in love, get engaged, and even conceive their children during the Dairyland.

They couldn't help but notice how the vibe at the Surf Classic was changing. The surfers they grew up with now used the event to introduce their kids to the Sheboygan surfing scene, including Tom Ziegler, who brought his son Jamie to one of the earliest Surf Classics. The Dairyland's days of drunken, bikini-clad women and foulmouthed, shirtless men partying along Broughton Drive had been replaced with parents pulling their kids in wagons and rolling along the sidewalk on tandem bicycles. As each kid signed up for his or her first paddleboard competition or was helped onto a longboard in time to ride his first Sheboygan wave, the weekend was becoming less about swapping beer-soaked surfing stories and more about being a part of the closely knit group of Great Lakes surfing tribes. To many of its loyal attendees, the Surf

Classic had become a tradition not to be missed, like baseball's opening day or Super Bowl Sunday.

"People have asked if we want it to become the Sturgis of surfing," Larry told a friend who asked about what the future holds. "Sturgis started out as nothing more than a little motorcycle party and look how that has exploded."

"At the same time, we wonder why we keep doing it. Most years we don't break even," Lee added. "We keep thinking about giving it to the Kiwanis or the Rotary so someone could develop it into a sandcastle-building competition or a Midwest surf-music festival."

Realizing that in their current state of exhaustion, mixed with a few beers, their feelings about hosting the Dairyland Surf Classic were not to be trusted, Larry said, "We'll wait until March when we've lost our suntans, are frozen under a foot of snow, and can clearly decide what we want to do."

Lee then finished his brother's thought: "No matter how it goes, one way or another, the next year's Dairyland Surf Classic will always be a success to look forward to."

The recent interest in the event stemmed mostly from their efforts to put Sheboygan on the international surfing map, which was never more evident than when they attended the San Luis Obispo International Film Festival earlier that year. On Thursday night, March 13, Lee and Larry were invited to help honor ninety-six-year-old filmmaker Bud Browne, the pioneer of surf films. As the annual Surf Night event was about to get under way, the brothers walked into the sold-out Fremont Theater to find two seats reserved for them in the second row. The brothers couldn't help but stargaze as they were surrounded by some of the biggest names in surfing, such as Peter Cole, John Peck, Joel Tudor, Linda Benson, Jack McCoy, Herbie Fletcher, Walter Hoffman, Fred Van Dyke, and surf journalist Steve Pezman.

The 2008 San Luis Obispo International Film Festival Surf Night celebration. From left to right: Lee Williams, Dana Brown, Dave Cole, and Larry Williams COURTESY OF ALAN FRASER

They were surprised to see some of those surfing legends gazing right back and whispering, "Aren't those the guys from *Step into Liquid*?"

As the biggest names in international surfing settled into their seats, the first autograph seeker chose the twin brothers from Sheboygan to approach.

"You're Sheboygan's Larry Williams!" the man said.

Larry calmly replied, "Yes, I am, and this is my brother Lee."

The guy then unrolled the Surf Night poster he had bought in the lobby moments earlier and asked the brothers to autograph it.

"With all the famous surfers in this theater, you want *our* autographs?" Lee asked.

As they finished signing the poster, Lee and Larry saw Bruce Brown and his son, Dana, seated near them. The brothers gave them a friendly wave, which the Browns returned.

Lee and Larry Williams finally meet the legend, Gerry Lopez. COURTESY OF
ALAN FRASER

As the lights dimmed for the start of the film, a gentleman
with black bushy eyebrows, salt-and-pepper hair, and well-de-
fined facial lines from years in the sun, turned around in his seat
and said, "I know you two."

"You do?" Lee whispered, his voice cracking.

"You're those guys who surf Sheboygan," he said, reaching
over the back of his seat to shake hands. "I'm Gerry Lopez."

Although the movie began with a stirring soundtrack followed by images of waves, sunsets, and bikini-clad women, Lee
and Larry would never be able to recall it. All they remembered
was the moment when one of their childhood idols had gone
out of his way to introduce himself to them. After honoring Bud
Browne, Lee and Larry attended the big Surf Night reception
held a few blocks away from the theater. Admitted for free along
with all the surfing legends and notables in attendance, they proceeded to enjoy the reception's hors d'oeuvres, refreshments, and
surf-band music. As most of the biggest names in surfing congregated in a corner to talk among themselves, the Williams brothers

chatted with their longtime friend Dave Cole, who was one of the festival's organizers. They tried to discuss the state of surfing in the world, but photographers and autograph-seekers interrupted them constantly. David quickly became the talent coordinator, trying his best to manage all of the requests.

As the night wound down, Gerry Lopez walked up to Lee and Larry. "You know, the best part of *Step into Liquid* was seeing you guys in Sheboygan," Gerry said. "I see a lot of surf films, and they're all kind of the same, but you brought something unique and different. It's great to see that's what you guys are all about."

The brothers talked to their idol for a while, feigning ease but still feeling like the teenage boys who had idolized him back in the days when they were mere gremmies hanging around outside the Lake Shore Surf Club's garage in Sheboygan and hoping someday to be recognized as genuine surfers. When the bartender dimmed the lights to signal that the party was over, Lee and Larry said good-bye to Gerry Lopez, still not quite believing they had met him and been treated as equals.

Dave, who had witnessed the entire exchange with Gerry, tried putting the night into perspective. "How do you get to the point in life where you're recognized by the biggest names in surfing?" he asked.

The boys shrugged. They felt as amazed as their friend.

"As a kid," Dave said, "you read the magazines, and if you were lucky, you got to see a guy like that in a movie. So just to see them in person would be a thrill. But they're coming up to *you* and putting their arms around *you* and asking for a photo."

As Dave walked with the Williams brothers to their car, Larry turned to Lee and said, "Through the years, our surfboards have carried us over the tallest waves and kept us afloat in the roughest waters."

Lee smiled and replied, "It's definitely been the ride of a lifetime."

Fourth Wave

Chapter Ten

It was a cold autumn morning in 2012. A thick fog hung atop the white-capped waves crashing against the idle shore of Lake Michigan. At the edge of the stone-lined pier that jetted out from the sandy Sheboygan beach, Lee and Larry Williams stared east toward the horizon. Neither said a word to each other, but both knew what the other was thinking.

We just hosted our last Dairyland Surf Classic.

What began in 1988 as a casual excuse to reunite a bunch of surfing buddies over the Labor Day weekend had evolved into a full-blown organized event two-and-a-half decades later. For years, the adrenaline rush they experienced from hosting the largest gathering of freshwater surfers in the world was second only to riding an actual wave. Their unwavering dedication to the three-day event attracted surfers from all the major Great Lakes surfing organizations. Even surfers from as far away as Honolulu and Australia attended the annual extravaganza because Lake Michigan was on their bucket list of places to surf before they died.

Over the years, Lee and Larry Williams's brazen embrace of their hometown's extreme surfing conditions earned them acclaim, credibility, and respect among those within international surfing circles. When they traveled, complete strangers would

A packed Sheboygan beachfront during the 2008 Dairyland Surf Classic
COURTESY OF WILLIAM POVLETICH

approach them to exclaim, "Hey, I know you—you're those crazy guys who jump off icebergs!"

That grassroots admiration was always appreciated, earning an aw-shucks guffaw from either of them in response: "I guess that's quite an accomplishment for a couple of teenagers who just wanted to surf in Sheboygan."

But even today, despite Lee and Larry's cult status, most of Sheboygan's 50,000 residents are unaware of their community's popularity as an internationally respected surfing destination. Ask any number of shop owners along Indiana Avenue or coffee drinkers at the Weather Center Café about the area's thriving surf scene, and they'll likely scoff, "You can't surf on Lake Michigan."

The Williams brothers and their Sheboygan surfing brethren have spent a lifetime debunking that perception with both tangible and intangible results. Word of their exploits has carried far beyond the fraternity of surf fanatics and wave riders. Not long ago, Larry was strolling along the lakefront when he came across a man in a tuxedo, his toes in the sand. The man, a doctor from Boston, had just driven up from a wedding in Milwaukee, explaining that he made the hour drive north because he couldn't believe people actually surfed in Sheboygan.

Larry, always the generous host, considered the circumstances to be an ideal opportunity to extend his distinct brand of Midwest hospitality. "Wanna borrow a wetsuit?" he offered. "It's in the car, along with an extra board, too."

The doctor was beside himself, graciously accepting the offer. For the next three hours, Larry taught him how to surf freshwater waves. They were having a blast. Only the encroaching dusk forced them to stop. When the doctor asked why Larry was being so generous, Larry replied, "What's the point if you can't share it?"

That lifestyle approach was embedded into Lee and Larry's personalities long before they learned how to surf. Since they were children, the brothers loved the lake; they still recollect with fondness the strolls taken with their parents around the North Point Lighthouse only a few blocks from their childhood home. Surfing provided them the vehicle to express their love of the water, even if they didn't realize how at the time. From the moment they started hanging outside the garage of the Lake Shore Surf Club, surfing provided their lives with purpose. It may sound shallow at first, but their motivations were rooted deeply in a spiritual foundation.

Their passion focused on a common interest, driving them to learn and succeed at something like never before. First, it was researching how to build a surfboard. Then it was learning how to read weather forecasts based on their surfing needs. Their ambition directed them to find the best wave formations along the Sheboygan lakefront, regardless of how far the trek was from their house. As they grew older, Lee and Larry started to articulate how surfing symbolized their approach toward life: "All life should be lived as if you're on the beach. Keep a positive attitude. Wear comfy clothes. Always be aware of your surroundings. Respect nature. Maybe you get inconvenienced when finding sand in your hair, or getting sunburned one day. But it's the beach. How bad can it be? You're living the dream."

For them, their pursuit of that dream began when they dragged their ten-foot wooden surfboard, complete with a rubber plug in the nose and a big wooden rudder on the bottom, into the forty-degree water of Lake Michigan on a cold winter afternoon. Underdressed for the brutal winter conditions in denim jeans and sweatshirts, and ignoring the early signs of hypothermia, they were determined to surf that afternoon, even after watching their kook board take on water quicker than the Titanic. When they finally found their balance atop the board, they rode their first of countless thousands of waves into shore, which is when both of them shared the same prophetic premonition: "I'll remember this day for the rest of my life."

Five decades later, that exact moment in time is still recognized as the catalyst for the path Lee and Larry still navigate. Although born during a more innocent time, their love of surfing provided them with the tools to live their lives to the fullest despite more than a fair share of tragedy and crisis. With the loss of that innocence came experience. Because of surfing, they were able to adapt the same techniques used to ride atop unpredictable waves when they faced difficult times in their lives, such as divorce or death. Their keen sense of balance, on and off a surfboard, helped them recycle every failure, disappointment, and setback into a steppingstone toward future success. As with the opportunity to ride a perfect wave, they learned to take nothing for granted. It's that approach that has them reveling in the benefits, seen in the loving relationship Larry shares with his wife Kerry and their daughter Mady, and in Lee's unconditional support toward his son Trevor's dream of becoming a renowned chef.

Although Lee and Larry never went looking for adversity, it always had a way of finding them. Even in high school, when

On New Years Day 2010, Lee heads to his car after another successful day of surfing.

only a few Sheboygan residents had heard of the Lake Shore Surf Club, most dismissed the group as nothing more than a band of rebellious misfits and their love of surfing as little more than a fad. On Friday, June 21, 1968, the Lake Shore Surf Club's existence in obscurity ended, appearing on the national consciousness thanks to a *Time* magazine article entitled "Students: Sniffing the Devil's Presence." The article, which detailed the goings-on of Students for a Democratic Society, stated: "If there was one common new goal it was a drive to expand S.D.S.'s influence in the nation's high schools. The Madison, Wis., chapter will try to do so this summer by publishing a state-wide underground newspaper aimed at teenagers [and] sending a 'radical rock-'n'-roll band' to tour youth-recreation spots. It even hopes to 'radicalize' a surf club in Sheboygan." Although Lee, Larry, and the rest of the Lake Shore Surf Club members appreciated the recognition, they had no idea who or what that group was all about or what the politics of Students for a Democratic Society had to do with them. Regardless, that didn't keep them from enjoying the thrill of being mentioned in a nationwide news article.

As they grew older, life changes rolled in like the fluid waves of Lake Michigan. Difficulties arose during the ride. Even when faced with the loss of family, they struck balance by applying their surfing skill sets, which allowed them to adjust to even the most unpredictable incarnations of a rolling wave. In all cases, it was about making the best of whatever came their way. For them, the prize was never about looking good on the smoothest of rides. Rather, it was in how they acclimated and survived by staying on their feet atop the most volatile waves, aware that success was not dependent solely on one's talents or abilities.

Nearly fifty years later, those same tumbling, white-capped waves were now crashing at the feet of Lee and Larry, pulling them out of their fond recollections. As they stood at the edge of the stone-lined pier, instead of basking in the glow of the Dairyland's twenty-fifth anniversary, they were trying to keep from being pushed over the edge by exhaustion. Each year the event got bigger, with increased workloads and rising expectations. It had become a year-round job. With increased popularity surrounding the event came an exponential avalanche of demands—be it from corporate sponsors, national media outlets, or simply their own desire to host the perfect weekend. Surfing was now providing

Lee and Larry Williams, still surfing in Sheboygan after nearly five decades.

Sheboygan with paybacks beyond the financial impact, benefiting local hotels, restaurants, and gas stations. Everyone wanted to be a part of the Williamses' internationally-renowned extravaganza. When the Sheboygan and Wisconsin boards of tourism began promoting the event with billboards, paid advertisements, and feature articles in several of their publications, the irony of such civic support wasn't lost on Lee, who remarked to his brother, "It's funny how life works. We first got into surfing to rebel against the system. Now we're a *part* of the system."

A few days after the twenty-fifth Dairyland, the reality that they were now involved in a complex bureaucracy presented itself to the grass-root founders when city officials offered to coordinate parking, permits, and promotion. Lee and Larry didn't need to debate or discuss the offer. Both had felt the realization brewing in their hearts for some time: "We never wanted to do this as a committee. It was always going to be run by us and only us. No thank you." And with that, the Dairyland Surf Classic was over. No fanfare, no press release, no tears shed.

Critics thought the Williams boys' surf party would go down in a blaze of controversy. Their friends thought it would live forever. All Lee and Larry cared about was ending the Dairyland on their own terms, just as they had started it twenty-five years earlier.

In the years since the Dairyland ended, Lee and Larry have been approached numerous times to re-launch the event. They've refused, even declining increased sponsorship offers and civic assistance to ensure greater success. Those they decline have accused them of surfing in so much cold water over the years that they're brain damaged, having lost the ability of rational thought. "It can be argued we never had any to begin with because we chose to step into Lake Michigan with a surfboard in the first place," Lee joked in response to the accusations.

But surfing in such frigid temperatures has also brought the brothers clarity. They had nothing left to prove. After five decades, they had tackled and conquered nearly every major and minor life obstacle with the support of Lake Michigan's crystal blue waters. If surfing was about finding balance atop a rolling wave, maneuvering until comfortable and secure, they were each still standing on their own two feet. If surfing was about trusting Mother Nature and respecting her power, they had stopped flirting with her wrath years ago. If surfing was about camaraderie, they had become distinguished ambassadors to a unique brotherhood of Great Lakes surfers. Their legacy helped influence a whole new generation of Midwestern surfers—many of whom chose to "share the stoke" through modern technology.

Across the Great Lakes, several aspiring filmmakers have followed Vince Deur's documentary masterpiece, *Unsalted:*

A Great Lakes Experience, with their own compelling and entertaining perspectives on the obsession and addiction of surfing in the Midwest. Scott Ditzenberger and Darrin McDonald's 2009 documentary film, *Out of Place,* features Lake Erie's chocolate-milk-colored waters while exploring the diverse and dedicated personalities of those who surf off the coast of Cleveland, Ohio, from lawyers to artists to factory workers. When Australians Jonno Durrant and Stefan Hunt were on a mission to surf in each and every one of the fifty states for their film, *Surfing 50 States,* they found Sheboygan personified the theme of their movie that no matter where you live, with a bit of creativity, you can always live your dream.

A search for "Great Lakes surfing" on YouTube is guaranteed to provide an endless array of the internet's most unusual surfing clips. With today's cell phones doubling as high-tech video cameras, it seems anyone can film themselves or their friends riding a wave. However, the video "Year End Swell" by Erik Wilkie and Hunter Rumfelt goes beyond just capturing the visual, proving that Minnesotans rank among the hardiest of winter warriors. Shot at Stoney Point, a popular surf break north of Duluth, the action captured in the six-and-a-half-minute movie torments all five senses of those brave enough to endure below-zero temperatures to ride big waves on Lake Superior, as well as the imaginations of those watching at home. One can't help but shiver when watching the surfers who, wearing thick wetsuits, surf for hours before walking back to their cars with ornate icicle formations dangling from their faces. Somehow these filmmakers make the sound of 38-degree water feel so downright arctic that the idea of a polar bear floating by on an iceberg wouldn't be immediately dismissed by viewers as a computer-generated special effect. And don't even try to imagine the smell created when they head into their idling cars to warm up between sets of waves.

The internet is full of information when it comes to freshwater surfing. One of the most frequented destinations for those aspiring to surf Lake Michigan is the website www.surfgrandhaven. com. Founded and maintained daily by a group of dedicated surfers from Grand Haven, Michigan, the site features marine forecasts, daily weather reports, updated water conditions, and a corporate-sponsored webcam that showcases the latest views along the Lake Michigan shoreline. And there's no shortage of available merchandise for those aspiring to become Great Lakes surfers. For nearly a decade, Ryan Gerard and his Third Coast Surf Shops in New Buffalo and St. Joseph, Michigan, have been spreading the joy of the Great Lakes surfing lifestyle, ensuring the latest surfboard technology and clothing lines are accessible in person and online. If you find yourself on the other side of the pond without a paddle, the EOS Surf Shop in Sheboygan is second-to-none when it comes to preparing the dedicated surfer or standup paddle boarder to catch the ride of a lifetime.

It's only fitting that the birthplace of the oldest international surf club on the Great Lakes happens to host one of the most active forums where those who surf along the coasts of Lakes Huron, Ontario, Michigan, Erie and Superior speak their minds and share their experiences. The Wyldewood Beach Club, located on the sandy shoreline of Lake Erie in Port Colborne, Ontario, Canada, also hosts an annual Eastern Surfing Association (ESA) contest where their famous longboard breaks test both a surfer's ability and resolve when riding the waves in their notoriously cold waters.

The internet has mobilized and united Great Lakes surfers like never before, providing a way for surfers from all around the Great Lakes to connect through social media outlets such as Facebook, Twitter, and Instagram. In 2008, when a Lake Michigan surfer was arrested in the shadows of the Windy City's iconic skyline,

Mitch McNeil spearheaded a powerful media response to bring attention to the injustice. With the help of evening newscasts and internet bloggers, the story of an innocent waterman falling victim to an outdated city ordinance captured the public's attention, swaying the court of opinion to weigh heavily on city officials until they proceeded to lift the ban. Today, selected city beaches along Chicago's Lake Shore Drive, including Osterman, Montrose, 57th Street, and Rainbow, are open for surfing. Meanwhile, McNeil continues to be an influential advocate for surfer's rights as the chapter president of Chicago's Surfrider Foundation.

During their five decades of surfing along the Great Lakes, Lee and Larry have visited all the major hotspots, frequenting several of them on a yearly basis back when their bodies could endure the frigid conditions on a daily basis. Having so much experience on such a large variety of breaks has given them additional clarity.

For surfing, wind is the primary wave-producing component on these inland freshwater oceans. When dragged over long stretches of Lake Michigan, the wind pulls up ripples and slants on the surface. Those irregularities become exaggerated, growing steeper and even more receptive to wind drag, rising like sails to collect more energy. The energy of the swells bonds together and travels in groups of waves called sets. Surfers look for patterns, gathering vital information by counting the number of waves in each set, noticing where the waves break and the length of the lulls between sets. Patience is a virtue when determining which wave to choose.

Oftentimes the fourth wave in a set is the most anticipated and largest, but also the most treacherous. Some winds aren't strong enough to transfer the needed energy into the water, resulting in waves that swell large at the beginning of a set, but then dissipate as they travel to shore. Other sets may benefit from a strong low-pressure storm system to create stronger, bigger, and more consistent waves per set. Lee and Larry always held out for the fourth wave. For them, it's always been the most rewarding.

In the thickening fog that hung atop the white-capped Lake Michigan waves on that cold autumn morning in 2012, Lee and Larry struggled to count the number of swells in each set. From their perch on the stone-lined pier that jetted out from the sandy Sheboygan beach, visibility was almost zero. In the past, they would have been in the water on surfboards the moment they awoke to such adventurous conditions. Nowadays, they opt to watch from the sidelines more often than not.

In recent years, the rigors of age have reminded them on several occasions that they are surfing on borrowed time. A few years ago, Lee almost lost more than his board to a raging set of waves that pulled him under multiple times. Larry needed to only look down at his self-proclaimed "Milwaukee Tumor"—what most would term a "beer gut"—to realize age and a slowing metabolism were catching up to him. The difference between the brothers and those finely tuned athletes who ignore Father Time is that Lee and Larry respect how their lives hang in the balance. When the bodies of athletes start to break down, they can walk off the field. If Lee and Larry weren't careful, they'd end up floating into shore.

The thrashing Lake Michigan waves—rushing and hurdling against one another toward land—kept taunting the reluctant surfers with an inviting wink. Their rationale said to stay put, but their senses were being assaulted and persuaded otherwise. They could smell the swells rolling past. Their faces tickled from the condensation of the crashing waves. Their ears could hear everything—from the traffic passing by on Broughton Drive to a group of teenage surfers experiencing Lake Michigan's unapologetic water temperatures for the first time. Their awed reactions echoed those of the Williams brothers four decades earlier.

Although the teens were outfitted with modern, state-of-the-art wetsuits and longboards, Lee and Larry admired their resiliency and determination that morning. For several years, they had considered the prospect of passing along the golden trident of Sheboygan surfing to the next generation. They just didn't know when. At that moment, the sun began to peek through the foggy haze, illuminating the Sheboygan shoreline in shades of orange and pink and the handful of Sheboygan's most determined teenage surfers standing at its edge with longboards nestled under their arms. The swoon of the surf was inviting them to play, just like a siren's song attracting an eager pirate. Lee and Larry, with their eyes once again fixed on the horizon, heard it too as they watched the youngsters patiently await the next great wave.

"Want to grab our boards out of the car?" Lee asked his brother.

"Of course! We might be old," Larry chuckled, "but we still like it cold."

Acknowledgments

When I first learned of the Dairyland Surf Classic and how Lee and Larry Williams transformed Sheboygan into the Malibu of the Midwest, my reaction was, "Who surfs on Lake Michigan?!?!?!" Although I grew up just forty-three miles south of them in Mequon with Lake Michigan literally in my backyard, I never once considered surfing to be a rational form of recreation during even the muggiest of summer afternoons in Wisconsin.

Over the next few years, their freshwater surfing exploits continued to fascinate me from afar. But it wasn't until Paulo Leite, a lifelong California surfer, discovered I was from the same corner of the world as "those guys from *Step into Liquid*" and couldn't stop asking me questions about what it was like to surf Sheboygan. That's when I realized the Williams' story had a universal appeal beyond the novelty of surfing in the Midwest.

When first meeting Lee and Larry over a couple of beers (okay, maybe a dozen), I was flattered by how much they entrusted me with their story. As we collaborated on every phase of the book—from outlining the initial plot on a bar napkin that evening through each version of the manuscript as it evolved—their cooperation knew no bounds. Because of their generosity, this book truly defines what a team can accomplish.

After Lee and Larry introduced me to their family as if I were a lifelong friend, Kerry, Mady, Trevor, Teresa, and Cheri were willing to share their most embarrassing and intimate stories. Neighbors Rosie and Sarah Goltry, childhood friends Andy Sommersberger, Kevin Groh, and Teek Phippen, fellow Great Lakes surfers Bob "Doc" Beaton, Vince Deur, Jim Gardner,

Jamie Ziegler, Lester Priday, and Dave Cole, as well as dozens of other folks I had the pleasure of chatting with during the past few Dairyland Surf Classics, generously took time to share their favorite anecdotes, memories, and impressions of the Sheboygan surf scene.

As anyone who has had the pleasure of speaking with Lee and/or Larry knows, the brothers are never short on words, so I would be remiss if the transcription team of Barbara Krultz and Associates weren't applauded for efficiently and accurately transcribing the numerous hours of recorded interviews.

The journey this book took to find a permanent home at the Wisconsin Historical Society Press couldn't have had a happier ending. I've truly cherished the friendships I've made with the entire team through the years, from top to bottom. Thanks to the tireless efforts of the triple-K team of Kathy Borkowski, Kate Thompson, and Kristin Gilpatrick, my stories will continue to have an opportunity to take on a life of their own.

As someone who encourages collaboration in every phase of my life, I have received endless words of encouragement and guidance from numerous friends and mentors through the years. I'm grateful to those who continually offer their experience and expertise toward improving my writing, including Bill Brummel, Bob Buege, Raul Galvan, Jack Heffron, and Kate Thompson.

Finally, I would be remiss not to mention how my family—from Mequon to Coloma—continues to support all of my endeavors, especially my wonderful wife, Kate, and two boys, Jackson and Cameron, who fuel my passion for happiness each and every day.

About the Author

Native Wisconsinite William Povletich is the author of *Green Bay Packers:*
Trials, Triumphs and Tradition (Wisconsin Historical Society Press, 2012),
Milwaukee Braves: Heroes and Heart-
break (Wisconsin Historical Society
Press, 2009) and *Green Bay Packers:*
Legends in Green and Gold (Arcadia
Publishing, 2005) as well as numerous magazine articles including the
award-winning *Liberace: The Milwau-*
kee Maestro. The Emmy Award-nominated and Peabody Award-
winning documentary filmmaker also produced *A Braves New*
World for PBS's *Milwaukee Public Television*, E!'s *Botched*, and the
Food Network's *Trisha's Southern Kitchen*.

O'CONNOR PHOTOGRAPHY